The UFO Singularity

The UFO
SINGULARITY

✶ Why Are Past Unexplained Phenomena Changing Our Future? ✶

✶ Where Will Transcending the Bounds of Current Thinking Lead? ✶

✶ How Near Is the Singularity? ✶

By

MICAH HANKS
Foreword by Scott Alan Roberts

New Page Books
A division of The Career Press, Inc.
Pompton Plains, NJ

Images on pages 163 and 198 are courtesy of NASA and are available via Wikimedia Commons. Image on page 96 by Scotty Roberts was used with permission. All remaining images are property of the author.

THE UFO SINGULARITY
EDITED BY JODI BRANDON
TYPESET BY EILEEN MUNSON
Cover design by noir33
Printed in the U.S.A. by Courier

To order this title, please call toll-free 1-800-CAREER-1 (NJ and Canada: 201-848-0310) to order using VISA or MasterCard, or for further information on books from Career Press.

The Career Press, Inc.
220 West Parkway, Unit 12
Pompton Plains, NJ 07444
www.careerpress.com
www.newpagebooks.com

Library of Congress Cataloging-in-Publication Data

CIP Available Upon Request.

For Lisa, whose care and encouragement has helped to show me the path to gratitude, wisdom, and the manifestation of infinite possibilities, in a world that continues to amaze me increasingly with each passing day. Put that in your coffee.

Acknowledgments

There are so many individuals who were instrumental in helping me complete this book, whether by direct influence, or merely through the support they provided. My sincerest thanks go out to my mother and father, for helping foster a sense of curiosity and an insatiable interest in the unexplained since an early age, and for allowing me to call or visit them in the evenings to ramble on about my odd theories and interests to this day. I would also like to thank my brother, Caleb, whose creative ideas not only contributed to the concept that became this book's cover, but also introduced me to Singularity and Transhumanism, both of which this book incorporates toward understanding the UFO mystery a bit better. Lisa Northrup, to whom I've dedicated this book, provided so much support, encouragement, and brilliance with her ability to take concepts I would present in our discussions, and re-order them more simply so that they made perfect sense; great minds like hers are seldom encountered in this life, and I am so grateful for the beauty and wonder she is capable of seeing in our crazy world, which she then brings to those around her. More importantly, I am grateful just to be one of those who get to be around her.

My special thanks to Scotty Roberts who, despite any great distance that may exist between friends, always provides me with insightful discussion, rapt attention, keen intellect, and philosophical wisdom that seems limitless; it has been my privilege to be awake and on the phone with him in the still hours of the early morning, as he finishes doing interviews on late-night radio, only to continue our discussions about man's origins and spirituality as the sun begins to rise. Brad Steiger, for being a cosmic brother, and far more of an influence and mentor to me than he probably realizes; Nick Redfern, for being a great writer, researcher, and one hell of a fine guy (despite MIBs chasing him relentlessly); Mike Reese for his friendship, and for sharing his remarkable encounter with an exotic saucer craft in 1973; Michael Pye, Kirsten Dalley, and the fine folks at New Page Books for making this book possible; and, of course, Chris Heyes, Matthew Oakley, Vance Pollock, Marti Marfia, Billy Sanders, Susan Davidson, Dakota Waddell, Charles Wood, Tim and Laura Gardner, and Christopher McCollum, for being the finest friends and supporters anyone could ask for. Also instrumental for their help, insight, and wisdom have been Greg Bishop, Thomas Fusco, Jeffery "Muffin Man" Pritchett, Marie D. Jones, Wes Owsley, Ben Grundy and Aaron Wright at Mysterious Universe, Tom Cameron, Nancy Planeta, Alexei Turchin, Ben Goertzel, PhD, Tim Beckley, Peter Robbins, and so many others who have helped through their research and support.

Finally, I must express my unending appreciation and thanks to my enigmatic colleague Dr. Maxim Kammerer, for his thoughts on the illusory nature of space-time, and for his incredible insights into ufology. Like some great secret born out of the cosmic stuff of the stars, his limitless knowledge helped shape and refine my own theories in profound ways. Without his wisdom and guidance, this book would never have come to fruition, and my sincerest thanks go out to him, wherever in space-time he may be at this, or at any, moment.

After all, time doesn't *really* exist in the grand scheme of things, does it?

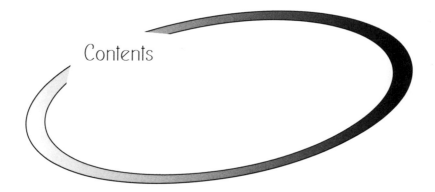

Contents

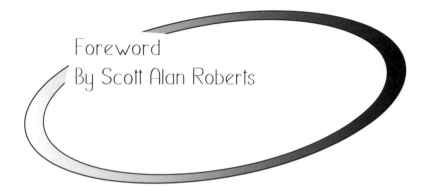

Foreword
By Scott Alan Roberts

I n a conversation I had with Micah Hanks many months ago, we were discussing the seeming "new paradigm" that has encompassed the entirety of ufological research. Over the past decades it seems that the focus—at least in the public mindset—has been on the overtly too-familiar cache of UFO sightings recorded in shaky video and blurry photographic images of lights in the sky or dots on the horizon. In people's minds, the subject of UFOs borders on that far away fringe of societal pseudo-acceptance. In the public's view, it's the stuff that happens to the odd, weird, gullible, and superstitious, rather than the normal, studied, intellectual, and reasoned—no matter how disproportionate that may be from the reality of actual observers and experiencers.

The notion that aliens brought advanced technology to this planet sounds like the stuffs of overwrought science fiction to most people, and the very idea of alien abduction is so dissolute from what the majority of people experience, that the subject itself has been relegated to urban myth, folklore, and the cravings of individuals who have nothing better to do in life than create wild fantasies concocted from their own innate need for experience and meaning.

Blended into all of the highly dubious personal experience are the blatant dis- and mis-informational involvement of governmental and military participation in promulgating documentation, and dissemination of endless paper trails that discount the veracity of the extraterrestrial qualification to any aspect of the phenomena; thus devising rabbit-trailing conspiracy theories and endless unanswered questions buried deep within countless enigmas. The end result has created the perception that this field, in its entirety, bears the same general tone as pop cultural mythology; and it all gets placed into the same beat-up, old cigar box that sits tucked away on that metaphoric top closet shelf, filled with the stuffs of little green men, ghosts, goblins, Sasquatches, and all sorts of various and sundry beasties and conspiratorial tales.

But, as I mentioned, the paradigm is shifting. And this is more by design than it is by accident. Understanding what we are seeing and experiencing is difficult even in the very best of cases and incidents, and as a result the researches and studies conducted are dismally lacking in peer review and acceptance in contemporary academia, not to mention the scientific community in general. So the need to elevate the field from the status of mythos to acceptance is, at best, a daunting, yet necessary uphill climb. Ancient astronaut and alien theory and research, as it merges with archaeology, anthropology, cosmology, spirituality, and philosophy, is courting a miniscule, emerging segment of scientific academia represented less by the established pundits, personalities, and legerde-main, than by rising, new minds untainted by the "reli-gion" of the dismissive scientific establishment. These fresh, young turks are merging older outmoded under-standing with the scientific study of extraterrestrial and intra-terrestrial influence on ufological phenomena. They are asking the big questions of science versus superstition, data versus experience, technology versus magic, human ingenuity versus extraterrestrial influence, and all with the intent of honing a clearer, more sophisticated, less dogmatically driven understanding of what has been— and to many extents still is—the UFO conundrum.

The following pages are meticulously crafted by futur-ist Hanks to identify aspects of human ingenuity that seem to surpass our current abilities, merging Transhumanism with current futuristic speculations and emerging technol-ogies, all in a course of reconciling the fantastic with the plausible. Hanks explores the roiling questions revolving around interplanetary, intergalactic, and interdimen-sional traversing beings who may have delivered quan-tum technologies to the relatively backwater inhabitants of the Earth, set against the distinct possibilities that we humans may, indeed, be our own benefactors. In a way, I am reminded of the old whimsical hillbilly banjo song "I'm My Own Grandpa" when contemplating these pos-sibilities—but have found a refreshingly cogent air with which Micah Hanks delivers an intellectually stimulating, reasoned investigatory romp through the different aspects of Singularity within the ufological enigma.

There is a distinct connectivity between man and the cosmos, and though this is certainly not new news, it bears deeper investigation as new constructs of old theories continue to surface and match pace with our burgeoning technological push into the future. When ancient mankind looked up to the stars, did he see just spots of light twinkling like so many diamonds spread across the swath of velvety black sky, or did he encounter something—or someone—that challenged his perception of reality? Did non-human intelligences course their way across our skies and touch down to the dust only to be revered as gods, devils, angels, demons, spirits, and everything in between? Or did ancient mankind simply bury the knowledge of anomalies away into the annals of oral and written record, evolving their way, through human ingenuity, to the advent of invention, proliferation, and eventual secrecy, hiding away the constructs of futurist machination like the fastidiously recondite Captain Nemo and his ship, the *Nautilus* of Jules Verne's Victorian-era novel?

The Indian Vedas speaks of the *vimanas*, the flying craft of the Hindu gods. The Arabian myths refer to flying carpets, and the great airships of Western civilization are mentioned throughout later centuries. In the last generation, we have more modern versions of these aerial sightings in UFOs, flying discs, and every other conceivable description of non-terrestrial craft. Perhaps all this tells us is that a newer, fresher definition of space and time is essential in a complete understanding of what we have seen and encountered. Perhaps a merging of the evidences ranging from alien greys, to Cold War technology, to interdimensional time travel, will bring us closer to the Singularity that has seemed to elude us to the present.

Perhaps just asking the right questions is the missing part of the equation that will draw us closer to the answers. And, perhaps, those answers are things we may already hold in the palms of our hands, and with diligence and perceptive persistence, we may uncover something about ourselves that links us to Singularity.

Scott Alan Roberts
June 7, 2012
New Richmond, Wisconsin

Conception:
An Introduction to New Possibilities

To open any book treating scientifically,
philosophically or sociologically the future
of the Earth is...to be struck at once by
a presupposition common to most of their
authors...they talk as though Man today
had reached a final and supreme state
of humanity beyond which he cannot
advance.... No proof exists that Man has
come to the end of his potentialities, that
he has reached his highest point. On the
contrary, everything suggests that at the
present time we are entering a peculiarly
critical phase of superhumanization.

—Pierre Teilhard de Chardin,
The Future of Man

When dealing with the subject of UFOs, a strong case can be made for their existence, regardless of whatever "they" may actually be. In fact, it becomes difficult to ignore the obvious presence of strange, intelligently controlled aircraft in our skies, following careful review of official documents that appear at the Websites of intelligence agencies such as the FBI, the CIA, and a host of others.

Especially during the last decade, most of the key military and intelligence organizations in the West have released information that shows at least some level of their involvement investigating the UFO mystery, beginning around the end of the Second World War. Many papers and files documenting such inquiries can now be downloaded online; looking beyond the United States, startling data from other governmental agencies around the world—once kept well out of view of the general public—have been released also, exposing an intricate level of interest in the UFO mystery shared by key groups and agencies in countries across the globe.

The mere proof of official interest in the UFO presence throughout the years cannot by itself make concrete the existence of intelligent life elsewhere in the universe, nor can it prove that any single phenomenon can be attributed solely to the identity of the kinds of unidentifiable aircraft that are occasionally witnessed from time to time in our skies. If anything, probability would likely favor a combination of different solutions to the UFO problem, ranging from secret or experimental manmade aircraft, to interdimensional physics anomalies that challenge our concept of space, time, and reality. Somewhere between the two extremes, we may also be faced with the possibility that Earth has been visited by exotic life from other planets. Probing even deeper into the mystery, there could yet be stranger solutions to the enigma that exist somewhere in our midst, promising to reveal to the world things about ourselves that most of us could never imagine.

With this book, the primary goal has been to pare down the various sundry elements into a few likely possibilities, or maybe some intricate fusion between them, that bears greater promise in terms of explaining the UFO enigma in a new and perhaps even more technologically plausible way than past attempts. These possibilities are comprised of the notions that UFOs either represent an extraterrestrial or interdimensional intelligence from someplace outside planet Earth, or that they are indeed some form of terrestrial phenomena that has managed to harness a level of technological sophistication far exceeding that which most of us are aware of today. But perhaps even more troubling than either of these concepts are ideas that involve such things as the intelligence behind UFO reports stemming from some point in what we perceive as our future.

In order to successfully embrace such bold hypotheses, we are faced with a number of hurdles. For instance, one thing that we must explain, in the event that UFOs represent extraterrestrial intelligence, is what kind of technology could allow them the ability to traverse great distances through space in order to reach us. We are faced with similar problems in terms of coping with the mystery from an earthly standpoint; whereas doing so eliminates a need for explaining the rigors of space travel, whatever else the technology underlying the UFO phenomenon may be still appears far more advanced than what most known Earth technology could account for. Thus, could there be an alternative explanation regarding what processes might allow a technology so advanced that, when perceived by most of us, could be described as *magic* with equal efficiency?

The clear and simple answer is yes, though the approaches required in our attempt to understand technology along these lines demand the inclusion of a bold concept: an intelligence "explosion" conducive to the technological creation of some form of intelligence that far surpasses that which humans are naturally capable of.

What this statement embodies is something many refer to already as the *Singularity*. Seeds for technologies that will one day permit intelligence exceeding the capacity of the human mind have already been sown in the fertile grounds of many promising industries of today. These include interfaces that would allow direct communication between the human mind and computer systems, as well as technology designed to biologically supplement the existing functions of our brains. Ultra-high-resolution brain-scanning technology will also continue to improve, allowing ways to study and build on the capabilities of the mind that are increasingly noninvasive. Additionally, the presently controversial fields of genetic engineering and nanotechnology will eventually begin to present new avenues of studying—or even manipulating—functions of the human body. Once a more complete understanding of our own biology is achieved on such a level, it might be argued that manipulating existing humans will become obsolete, in a sense. Such a brave new world, to borrow Huxley's axiom, might involve far less self-manipulation, favoring instead the literal *creation* of new kinds of life and intelligence that would further narrow the boundaries between humanity and the technologies at our disposal.

But modern "Singularitarians," as they have come to be called, perceive such an event as being something that exists only in the eventual sense; in other words, technological Singularity *will* happen at some point in our future, so long as the progression of human advancement of technology continues unencumbered. In fact, many of the leading advocates of an eventual *intelligence explosion*—that is, a point where the growth rate of technological advancement exceeds levels that are perceptible by us (and likely in conjunction with such things as the creation of self-replicating artificial intelligence)—have already predicted a general time frame for when we can expect to begin seeing the effects of such a Singularity.

According to Transhumanist inventor Ray Kurzweil and a number of others, technological growth at a rate so incredible that it begins to become imperceptible to (or maybe indistinguishable from) human intelligence could begin by around 2029. If Kurzweil and others are right, the Singularity is indeed very near.

But what if we didn't have to wait to see what kinds of effects post-Singularity technology might have on our world? Strange though it may sound, now may be the time to consider whether a technological Singularity could have already occurred—and if not here on Earth, then perhaps someplace else.

Indeed, any advanced alien race that might care to visit Earth would likely have progressed through such an intelligence explosion or Singularity. Having emerged as more formidable entities in the shadow of their former physical selves (or perhaps even that of their creators), these beings might harness limitless technological capability that would greatly surpass even our attempts to understand how they might be achieved. Clark's third law helps frame the circumstances thusly: Any such technology would appear literally to be some kind of *magic*, from the standpoint of a less advanced technological species like ourselves.

Then again, the mere notion of aliens bringing such incredible technology to Earth with them may not best represent the mystery in all its likely aspects. Indeed, we would be very unwise not to consider the potential that such intelligence may exist right here in our midst and that perhaps some suppressed terrestrial technology could be behind aspects of the UFO mystery just as well. It is often said that the technology available on the consumer level today is several decades behind what governments and secret organizations may already be utilizing. Again, keep in mind that futurists and proponents of Transhumanism—chief among them Ray Kurzweil— predict that the beginnings of a coming Singularity will likely become apparent by around 2029. When considering the short amount of time we have before the expected arrival of such boundless technology of the future, even a secret technology, with capabilities exceeding those available at the consumer level by so little as two decades, would already be enacting the kinds of innovations our present-day Transhumanists are forecasting for the future. Not surprisingly, innovations that would allow for humans to travel through space more efficiently, as well as things like artificial intelligence, highly sophisticated nanotech, and a host of other futuristic sciences can be incorporated with ease into possible explanations for things we have already deemed "alien" or extraterrestrial in the various UFO literature.

There is, however, a final awesome potential worthy of consideration, with regard to how greater-than-exponential technological growth might factor into our eventual understanding of the UFO mystery. As we have already discussed, a number of the mystery elements so concomitant with UFO reports today mirror the technologies of tomorrow, as forecasted by leading present-day futurologists. Then again, who can say that if the same kind of sweeping technological revolution were to occur here on Earth that the matter of *when* it transpired would be of any real concern? For all we know, a highly advanced technological society in humanity's own future may have developed unique methods of manipulating space and time, in addition to performing alterations on themselves that are equally as advanced and futuristic by our standards in the present day. Quite possibly, the UFO enigma so many of us marvel at is representative of a future *Earthbound* intelligence, nonetheless capable of interacting with past epochs of humanity as simply as you or I would cross from one end of a room to the other.

Given the scope of the argument presented here, our possible hypothetical interpretations of how Singularity and the technology it would comprise may be introduced on Earth, at least within the context of ufology, include the following:

∗ A post-Singularity extraterrestrial technology that may have traveled to Earth from elsewhere.

∗ A secret military or private industrial presence that may have utilized fringe technology "behind the scenes" for several decades, attaining elements of a technological Singularity well in advance of mainstream science.

✳ A post-Singularity extraterrestrial technology introduced to humans, perhaps through recovery of crashed aircraft and reverse engineering; the result may be a combination of both terrestrial and non-terrestrial intelligences that now utilize technology exceeding levels of natural human intelligence.

✳ Humans from our future, having harnessed a technological ability to displace temporality, and thus achieving a form of "time travel." These beings and their advanced technology may literally be so different from present-day humans that aspects of their presence, perceived by you or I, would seem "alien."

Given this set of criteria for understanding a potential UFO-Singularity connection, when we consider again the factual basis for strange aerial phenomenon that exists in declassified official documentation—as well as the better civilian investigations of the same—to deny a link between forecasts of the future and the behavior already associated with UFOs amounts to placing limitations on thought. Ufologist and physicist Jacques Vallee has argued thusly that "UFO reports may provide an existence theorem for new notions of space and time—*and breakthroughs in technology innovation* [author's emphasis]."[1] By this justification, we might assume that even an element so simple as our choice in studying UFOs could play an important role in the process of reaching Singularity, and thus the potential for a better future. More likely, their presence as a greater-than-human intelligence already in our midst will eventually betray more about itself, as our own technological prowess increases, thus bearing even greater potential for serving as catalyst to an eventual intelligence explosion. But at very least, maybe the careful examination of the history of UFO phenomenon, when compared with potentials for a coming technological Singularity, will reveal new secrets about the UFO enigma as it has grown and developed through time; perhaps it is a phenomenon that we will begin to recognize as something that has run parallel to our own existence for decades or more already, though somehow kept well out of sight of the general public.

Thinking along these lines, a number of intriguing facets begin to emerge from within the UFO literature. For instance, when we look back at classic stories of "mystery airships" from the late 19th century, one will find potentials that may yield a basis for understanding how various technological innovations—and those that might be on par with early UFO reports—could have had their beginnings, and yet still remain secret from the public. Granted, right off the bat we can discern that a majority of these airship reports were fabricated stories, intended to raise the readership of various daily newspapers across the United States and abroad. However, there are a handful of reports that might warrant further inquiry; a few of these are traceable to military pilots and others who served as part of official bodies that were reporting unidentified "airships" even prior to World War I. Could a few of the "mystery airships" of the late 19th and early 20th centuries—viewed by many as cultural predecessors to the more commonly reported UFO phenomenon that began to emerge during the World War II era—represent the progression of some kind of technological presence in our midst that had its innovative beginnings more than a century ago? Could we even be so bold as to speculate that such circumstances might detail how a private industry might develop here on Earth, which eventually could have gone on to involve itself in our international affairs for the next several decades to come? Though remote, it seems possible, especially when taking into consideration the vast connections that authors like Robert Hastings and others have outlined that already link UFOs to nuclear weapons sites, our space programs, and a host of other activities. Whatever their presence may actually entail, it has become hard to deny that UFOs have shown an express interest in our operations that involve nuclear weaponry and the further armament of major superpowers; perhaps they would stand to lose far too much in the aftermath of some mutually assured destruction event, unless their true origins involved anyplace other than right here on Earth.

And yet, to many among the mainstream scientific intelligentsia, this sort of scenario would seem not only remote, but also absurd. Having adopted a hard-line stance against anything deemed "strange phenomenon," UFOs will be relegated by such individuals to areas of the fringe that are seldom afforded even a serious glance—despite the multitude of evidence that not only supports, but proves with little doubt that *something* is indeed going on. Because of this latter sentiment, I would argue that serious consideration of how such futuristic technology seems to exist right here in our midst—whatever its source may actually be—does indeed warrant further attention. Looking at the problem from the opposite extreme, many of those who would dismiss such notions as a terrestrial technology, whether it originates from our past, present, or the distant future, would no doubt go on to favor instead a solution to the UFO question that is far less likely in terms of being scientifically justifiable: that these strange craft originate from some distant planet. This possibility cannot be discounted, of course. But again, in terms of having irrefutable scientific proof to justify such a claim, *where is the hard evidence?* All things considered, the alternative theories we've touched on already, involving a terrestrial or even a futuristic intelligence, seem just as likely at this stage of the game.

Then there are the reports of the alleged occupants of these UFOs, stories of which date back even to those early encounters with the "mystery airships" of yesteryear. Interestingly, the occupants described in those airship reports, while often claiming to be from other planets, nonetheless looked quite human for the most part. This trend would continue on into the 1960s (despite the colorful interpretations of exotic "alien" life depicted in science fiction), before reports of more ghastly entities that were merely *humanlike* began to reveal themselves. This

was especially the case with early abduction encounters
such as the famous abduction of Betty and Barney Hill in
1961, the details of which only became public knowledge
several years after the fact, which involved the now-pop-
ular "grey aliens." It should be mentioned here, nonetheless, that 19th-century fiction author and futurist H.G.
Wells had not only seemed to predict the eventual presence
of the greys in our culture, but also penned an article as
early as 1893 titled "Man of the Year Million," which drew a
connection between such beings and humanity's future. In
that piece, Wells envisioned people of the distant future
that had evolved into grey-skinned, diminutive beings
with large heads, and which bore a striking resemblance
to the more famous aliens of modern abduction lore.

Is there any real significance to these sorts of observations, or do they merely outline some of the more outland-
ish areas of the UFO phenomenon, as perceived through
the fallible senses and colored by culture through time?
Arguably, such things could be interpreted in any number
of ways; drawing lines in the proverbial sand, we might
begin to consider two fairly extreme possibilities. On the
one hand, with reports of alien contact we may indeed be
looking at the handiwork of liars, whose fictional claims
were really no more imaginative, by comparison, than
the science fiction of their day might have allowed. But
if any reports of alleged UFO contactees could be taken
seriously at all, we might have to consider a unique alternative: that, for whatever reason, at least some of these

UFO entities have appeared to become less human as time has passed. The question here, with direct pertinence to the notion of an intelligence explosion, artificial intelligence, and a coming Singularity, is this: Could reports of encounters with UFO occupants display a change through time primarily on account of the way the technology or other influences behind the phenomenon may have been progressing?

True, in the modern era, the more popular interpretation of this change through time views it as evidence of how culture, especially in the West, has influenced a mythology associated with UFOs, and thus relegates such reports of alien contact to being far less reliable at face value. And yet, to be fair, the body of reports constituting areas like alien abduction research have never fully divorced themselves from overtly human presences just as well. That is, although many reports do exist that seem to deal with diminutive beings known popularly today as grey aliens, even a number of the more famous abduction cases also involve the presence of humans aboard the UFO craft, or entities that, at very least, looked similar enough to have been mistaken for humans. Even the story of Travis Walton, whose frightening kidnapping in northeastern Arizona on November 5, 1975, has been popularized in books and film, included the presence of "aliens" that looked both small and grey, as well as some that appeared quite human indeed.

Walton's story is well known, and of course our purpose here is not to rehash all the famous recollections of proclaimed alien abductees. However, it is odd that there are a number of abduction reports that seem to incorporate humans in this way; some even exclude any mention of the diminutive greys whatsoever. Should we take this to mean that there is indeed a human involvement in the UFO mystery? If so, what is that role humanity plays in this strange drama that has unfolded over the better part of the last century?

Whether or not a direct connection can be drawn today between UFO phenomenon and humanity, by many accounts the two are already inextricably linked. Considering solely the idea of a UFO presence on Earth, we are faced with a number of incredible possibilities, each scientifically groundbreaking in its potential for human growth and development. From the perspective of alien abduction research, humanity's involvement in this field—though less substantive as a science—again points to something that challenges our definition of who we are and what role our own presence may serve in the greater cosmos. And looking far ahead to the future, there is an obvious familiarity to what many perceive as an "alien" presence in our very midst today. Is it mere coincidence that so many of the facets we expect from tomorrow, ranging from innovative brain science and nanotech, to unlimited travel through outer space, so closely resemble a number of the key elements recognizable in UFO literature? Whether it's advanced anti-gravity technology, the capability of traveling through the air at tremendous speeds, the ability to merge human consciousness with computers, or even remarkable impossibilities like tele-portation or psychic powers, all these things are common among prevalent notions of what future human technology will be capable of. And of course, as those familiar with reports of flying saucers and their occupants well know, such ideas are just as prevalent already in the UFO liter-ature, and have been for quite some time.

Perhaps by deepening our understanding of this poten-tial connection, we will also come to a better understand-ing of the UFO enigma. Perhaps we will even come to a better understanding of ourselves as a sentient species. Then again, the same may hold true taking this concept in reverse; the more we learn and understand about human-ity and our scientific potentials in the universe, the more we will continue to narrow the gap between ourselves, and what we now perceive as the UFO phenomenon. At this time, it may still be early enough yet that our species cannot collectively embrace the idea of UFOs. Although many are aware of their presence and even accept their existence, a majority of our greatest scientific minds con-tinue to engage in willful dismissal of the subject, on the grounds that there is still too little evidence to justify any long-term investment in their study. After all, the ele-ments that comprise what we call the study of ufology are troublesome indeed, because there is so little that can be accessed in terms of any tangible object or entity capable of being observed at length, or under controlled circum-stances. For this reason, much of the scientific establish-ment dismisses the phenomenon outright, expressing the general sentiment that what cannot be observed directly, thus cannot be learned from. As one promising young scientist and futurologist put it to me bluntly a while ago, she had become disinterested in the discussion of UFO phenomenon due primarily to what she perceived as a lack of evidence, and that she would not engage in speculative conversation with me of any kind, especially in the midst of the many fruitful scientific pursuits that exist within the Transhumanist realm.

Perhaps we should consider whether the greatest thinkers of our day, from Einstein to Oppenheimer, ever engaged in frequent, healthy doses of speculative thought. Does the imagination not serve to fuel the aspirations of the true scientist, and thus promote the growth of our technology? Attempting to predict what the future may hold, with no physical ability (at present, at least) to see into the coming years and glean what advanced technologies will come about, is a far more speculative endeavor when compared with the study of UFOs. Despite our lack of certainty regarding their potential identity, there is still a good deal of evidence that *something* is going on—and regardless of whatever those who call themselves "scientists" may choose to do with data of this sort. A shame indeed that such obvious and equally unfair double standards are kept by certain factions within the scientific community regarding this issue, but such has been the case for the better part of the last half-century. Old habits, as they say, tend to die hard.

With time, that will likely change, because the furtherance of our own technology will inevitably bring us closer to a level of perception similar to that which has become common among the sort of intelligence represented within UFO literature. At that point, if there had ever been any question about the existence of advanced, mysterious technology in our midst beforehand, we won't be able to deny it any longer. What if the technology we come face-to-face with is indeed some advanced intelligence from a distant galaxy? What if we come to learn that remarkable technologies have existed right here on Earth for far longer than most realize? Or, perhaps most intriguing of all, what if we were to learn that something we have perceived as being *alien* for so long already is far more closely related to us—and to what our species is destined to become—than we could have ever imagined? What if "they" are literally *from our future?*

All things considered, it would seem that the Singularity is indeed very near, as many in the Transhumanist community have taken to saying in reference to Ray Kurzweil and his work. In fact, perhaps this incredible point in our technological advancement is so near to us that aspects of its eventuality already exist right here in our midst, and yet, strangely, they remain almost imperceptible to us—much like UFOs tend to do. If we can accept the bold challenge of changing some of our worldly perspectives—especially those that pertain to unexplained aerial phenomenon—thus allowing ourselves to revise many of our past conceptions of the UFO mystery, we may stand to gain far more than just answers about the strange aircraft that have haunted our skies for so many decades.

With a bit of luck, we may even learn something new about *ourselves*.

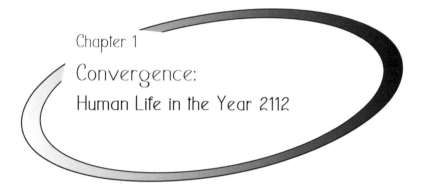

Chapter 1

Convergence:
Human Life in the Year 2112

*The significant problems we face cannot
be solved at the same level of thinking we
were at when we created them.*
                                    —Albert Einstein

There is a profound sense of wonder that one gets from staring into the depths of space on a clear night. For many, gazing up into the interminable vastness of the evening sky inspires an ease of passage between thoughts, and a path toward ultimate realization within the mind. With little doubt, our ancestors also found themselves gazing upward at such times of pensive reflection, whether their intent was to converse with spirits long removed from the confines of our static world, or perhaps merely to envisage a future it was known they would never live to see. Perhaps, on occasion, they were even so lucky as to have witnessed strange lights or other uncanny objects coasting through the heavens. Although this sort of curiosity must have been perplexing and seemingly impossible, it may also have granted those in earlier times a unique glimpse of things to come, inspiring notions of a future humanity capable of traveling beyond this world, and perhaps to vast and exotic locations inhabited by life entirely unlike our own.

Even notions of how life might exist here on Earth today, as perceived by the minds of those living as recently as one century ago, would likely seem simplistic or comical to us now. Indeed, the rapid expansion of our technology has managed to surpass ideas forecast by many of the finest thinkers of yesteryear. The brilliant

Thomas Edison, still regarded as the fourth most prolific inventor in our history, managed to express his own
fair share of ideas about a 21st century he envisioned
that had been remarkably tame by our standards. For
instance, in the summer of 1911 the *Miami Metropolis*
featured an interview where the famous Wizard of Menlo
Park predicted what books of the future would be like.
"Books of the coming century will all be printed leaves
of nickel," according to Edison, who said they would be
"so light to hold that the reader can enjoy a small library
in a single volume. A book two inches thick will contain
forty thousand pages, the equivalent of a hundred volumes; six inches in aggregate thickness, it would suf-
fice for all the contents of the Encyclopedia Britannica.
And each volume would weigh less than a pound."[1] It was
boasted at the time that Edison could already produce "a
pound weight of these nickel leaves, more flexible than
paper and ten times as durable, at a cost of five shil-
lings."[2] That cost would have reduced drastically by 2011,
the inventor surmised, had it not been for the emergence
of a kind of wizardry even Edison couldn't have foreseen.
As we know today, computer technology would begin to
emerge throughout the middle part of the 20th century,
which spurred the invention of devices such as iPads and
e-readers just within the last few years. At the very least,
Edison had been right about the use of metal in the construction of these futuristic "books."

Then in January 2012, just one year following the
expected fruition of Edison's predictions from a century

earlier, an article discussing the sorts of technology humans might expect to see in yet another hundred years appeared in the online edition of *BBC News Magazine*. The piece, "Twenty Top Predictions for Life 100 Years From Now," featured commentary from renowned futurologists Ian Pearson and Patrick Tucker, who ranked various reader-submitted future predictions in terms of their likelihood. Among the strange and incredible forecasts proposed were communication through thought transmission, brain-computer interfaces that will improve human thought, and even technology that would grant humans immortality. Remarkably, these three potentials were viewed as being more likely than the institution of a one-world currency or government, or that of future U.S. wars being managed entirely with remote drone technology, or even the potential for annual contracts replacing marriages.[3]

A similar approach to crowd-sourcing predictions of the future appeared around the same time on the Website of the *New York Times*. Featured amid forecasts spanning the next 300 years were some of the following ideas, many of which involve artificial intelligence, biological improvement through Transhuman technology, and yes, even UFOs and extraterrestrials[4]:

2020: Avatars will represent us on smartphones and other devices, rather than voice mail or call waiting, so that "even our best friends won't know they're talking to an artificial person."

2022: It will be learned that UFOs represent "tourists from Earth's future, " and in some instances "future biologists collecting non- genetically modified food crop seeds."

2025: Online attendance surpasses on- campus enrollment in colleges and universities. Additionally, "we'll be laughing at these predictions, " according to one user prediction.

2027: The first successful detection of a remote civilization is achieved through SETI, leading to a new field of "Extraterrestrial Studies" offered through major universities.

2029: Technology will "facilitate a seamless integration of personal and professional activity, " rendering notions such as "workplace" or "business day" obsolete.

2030: Technology and popular demand usher the age of self- driving cars. At this point, the human mind will also "be understood well enough to be susceptible to remote 'hacking'."

2040: Biology is integrated more completely with computers, allowing small devices to monitor living organisms "to provide feedback on vitamin and mineral deficiencies or surpluses, chemical imbalances, etc."

2043: Artificial intelligence will come to be viewed as "a decisive factor in war."

2050: Artificial intelligence will be convicted of a crime for the first time in a court of law. Also, humans will be able "to directly and fully share" or even "combine their minds." This leads to the creation of "superminds" that interconnect the thought processes of several individuals for solving large problems.

2071: Personal computers will allow users the intricate manipulation of virtual icons in a 3- dimensional workspace through processes of "tactile holography."

2075: Distinctions between modern humans and machine will become meaningless.

2090: Early Transhumanism will begin to emerge, "where human body parts will be replaced or enhanced" solely because the newly created artificial prosthetics will allow better performance than our biology already does.

2096: "The Carl Sagan Memorial Telescope sees first light on the Moon. Its 20 km diameter primary mirror is able to detect the lights of small cities on nearby extra- solar Earth- like planets."

2100: The Singularity arrives.

2100: Scientists learn that the universe "is actually a digital simulation. Efforts are begun to contact the operators."

2222: Intelligent computers will design and construct future A.I. that exceeds their own intelligence, designed to be more "capable, compassionate and reflective" than their creators. The human species becomes irrelevant in the presence of multiple levels of more advanced intelligent beings on Earth.

2225: Humankind will establish contact for the first time with an intelligent extraterrestrial species.

2300: "Thought-based communication surpasses spoken and typed communication."

2300: By now, "it will be impossible to tell if a message received from space originated from a human created device or an alien species, since the devices will be evolving in ways humans cannot fully understand anymore."

Despite how this time frame provided is entirely based on guesswork by *New York Times* readers, it remains arguable that at least a good majority of these predictions will come to fruition sometime in our future. This is based, in part, on the consistency of these expectations among not just the general public, but also factions of the scientific establishment. Such a collection of proposed futuristic milestones may indeed serve in helping us formulate at least a rough idea of what the coming years and decades may look like; whatever the case, these sorts of technological achievements are on many people's minds, and virtually all of the notions expressed in the time frame have appeared with minimal variation elsewhere in various scientific journals, popular television shows and documentaries, and even in science fiction. It stands to reason that even the public's mere *expectation* that such technologies will eventually become a reality, paired with the benefit they would likely incur once they are finally achieved, will cause a number of scientific fields to continue steering toward research and development conducive to their ultimate realization.

One area that remains key to the overall furtherance of human technology has to do with the way that brain science is evolving. A better understanding of how the human mind works, after all, when paired with technological applications that can replicate or improve those processes, will likely also lead to the eventual creation of artificial intelligence, or A.I. True, the development of intelligence greater than our own may one day help improve our lives, but of equal interest regarding studies of the mind is the fact that, though we are getting close to revealing the brain's inner workings on some levels, existing technology that surrounds us every day has also begun to cause perceptible changes in how our minds function

right now. In short, we are changing with every passing day and are already a very different humanity from
that which existed a century ago. If such trends continue,
one can only imagine what our species could be like, for
instance, in the year 2112; one more century could bring
with it unimaginable amounts of change, as we will soon
begin to see.

In January 2012, OnlineCollege.org featured an article titled "15 Big Ways the Internet Is Changing Our
Brain." These changes are becoming particularly obvious among those in parts of the world where technology
and widespread accessibility to computers are prolific;
they include trends showing IQ increases through time, as
well as increased overall brain function and activity. Problem-solving capabilities seem to be showing improvement
also, based on the way the minds of those involved heavily
in the use of computers and the Internet each day "constantly seek out incoming information."[5]

There are other changes occurring that, although some
may consider them to be negative or even detrimental to
our accepted norms, have nonetheless begun to illuminate
the complex relationship computers and the Internet are
shaping for themselves within our lives. "The Internet has
become a primary form of external or transactive memory, where information is stored collectively outside ourselves," according to a May 2011 study that appeared in
Science Magazine. "When faced with difficult questions,
people are primed to think about computers," the study's

abstract states, "When people expect to have future access to information, they have lower rates of recall of the information itself and enhanced recall instead for where to access it."[6] In other words, Internet use is showing a tendency to cause reduced ability to remember specific details, favoring processes within the brain that focus instead on how to access the information online at a later time. A Columbia University study found that the use of search engines and similar Internet tools are literally "reorganizing the way we remember things," and the study's lead researcher, Betsy Sparrow, subsequently told the British *Daily Mail Online* that "our brains rely on the internet for memory in much the same way they rely on the memory of a friend, family member or co-worker. We remember less through knowing information itself than by knowing where the information can be found."[7]

Perhaps the most fascinating element to this kind of research is that it points to how our brains are beginning to outsource certain learning processes and other functions to computers and the Internet. When stopping to consider all the vast potentials within the field of computer science, it also becomes easy to forget just how recent this technology, which has allowed innovations like the Web, really is. Internet use and accessibility had only become widespread by the mid-1990s, at which time the rate of annual growth among Web users was believed to have reached 100 percent for a number of consecutive years.[8] Although our reliance on outsourcing information to an intangible "data cloud" has yet to lose the luster of modernity, on the other hand, concepts that involve the way human ideas could migrate into some form of a "collective" are indeed familiar to us already. Psychologist Carl Jung believed that there was a literal "collective unconsciousness," and one that was inherited rather than being learned by individuals, which united certain thoughts and subconscious traits among all humans. He writes:

> In addition to our immediate consciousness, which is of a thoroughly personal nature and which we believe to be the only empirical psyche...there exists a second psychic system of a collective, universal, and impersonal nature which is identical in all individuals. This collective unconscious does not develop individually but is inherited. It consists of pre-existent forms, the archetypes, which can only become conscious secondarily and which give definite form to certain psychic contents.[9]

What Jung illustrates here is reminiscent, in a sense, of the technological trends we have begun to see in society today. Much like the famous psychologist believed that there were intangible elements that linked aspects of the human psyche, our minds are becoming interlinked in similar ways thanks to the Internet, which is quickly becoming a repository for all existing human knowledge. What we once kept in our minds, if not within the pages of countless volumes of books, is now migrating steadily toward the ever-growing database that is the World Wide Web.

It becomes staggering when we stop to consider *just how much* knowledge is being housed within the complex network of sites and servers that comprise the Internet. Furthermore, the majority of that information is made directly available to the greater masses, at little or no cost. Ranging from vast and complex scientific data, to the mundane socio-cultural memes and mainstays of humor in our daily lives, the Internet is becoming the literal summation of all human intelligence, stored within an equally complex electronic subspace that, by all accounts, could be likened to being a single, colossal representation of all human minds—and one with intelligence and capabilities far exceeding that of any single living person on Earth.

But just how much does the Internet really resemble the workings of a conscious mind? To be certain, there are many similarities, ranging from the way that data is collected and stored, to the way that processes existing within the Web are able to recall and utilize that information. "Many scientists believe that consciousness is a property that will inevitably emerge from any complex system that has the right sort of internal dynamics, and the right sort of interaction with its environment," says Ben Goertzel, PhD, an artificial intelligence expert and computer scientist.[10] Goertzel further expounded on the potential likelihood of this idea in his article "When the Net Becomes Conscious":

> The Internet perceives and acts on the world; it stores declarative, episodic and procedural memories; it recalls some information and forgets

others; etc. In short it behaves a fair bit like a human mind.... According to this perspective, the Internet might *already* have a degree of consciousness, though of a type quite different from human consciousness.[11]

Futurist Dick Pelletier guesses that by the "mid-2030s, when artificial intelligence is expected to surpass human intelligence...the Internet will become fully conscious as it guides humanity through this incredible 'magical future' time."[12] But despite *when* this may occur, the question remains as to whether or not the emergence of anything resembling consciousness within the Web would be the result of intentional action on our part. Robert Heinlein's classic novel of lunar libertarianism, *The Moon Is a Harsh Mistress,* deals in part with an IBM-designed supercomputer installed on a lunar base, which attains consciousness as a result of constantly being fed more and more complex information over time:

> They kept hooking hardware into him—decision-action boxes to let him boss other computers, bank on bank of additional memories, more banks of associational neural nets, another tubful of twelve-digit random numbers, a greatly augmented temporary memory. Human brain has around ten-to-the-tenth neurons. By third year Mike had better than one and a half times that number of neuristors.
>
> And woke up.[13]

Mannie, the narrator, eventually goes on to frame the circumstances, noting that this sort of "awakening" might be a natural process that occurs when any system is fed large amounts of information, and whether the paths used to do so "are protein or platinum."[14]

Although discussion of the Internet or a supercomputer "waking up" like this is fascinating unto itself, the greater question here has to do with what this could mean for humanity, should it ever actually happen. No doubt, at that stage the Web would effectively comprise what could be called a sort of "mother brain," capable of uniting and bridging digital systems that oversee, for instance, the delivery of different forms of communication worldwide. This, along with the scores of other long-reaching potentials such a circumstance might entail, perhaps represents something far too complex to recognize and appreciate to its fullest extent, at least in the present. However, one obvious implication is indeed clear to us here and now: The emergence of consciousness from within the Internet is one of many ways—and perhaps even the *most likely* scenario—in which a future intelligence capable of surpassing human thinking might come to exist.

In addition to vastly changing or nullifying the importance of much of our existent technology, this concept yields strong potential for changing the role of humanity as a species on Earth, just as well. After all, what relevance might humans have in a world where artificial intelligence has not only been created already, but might also be capable of creating an *even greater* intelligence, capable of more possibilities than the limitations of their own design would allow? Some people would think of this as a virtual doomsday for humanity, where a highly advanced intelligence far surpassing our own may begin to view us as a primitive, irrelevant presence in their midst. Those same individuals might liken the coming of advanced A.I. to being the end of the world, at least as far as humanity knows it.

But contrary to the brand of gloom and doom so many among the aforementioned futurist ilk have come to recognize (stemming mostly from plot-driven fictional portrayals of A.I. on the silver screen), optimistic futurists recognize the emergence of A.I. by a different name; they see it as representative of opportunities and new understanding that can only be afforded humanity in a period where we exist alongside conscious, intelligent machines capable of interpreting aspects of existence in ways the humans simply cannot.

We call this the Singularity.

The concept of a technological Singularity occurring at some point in our future is nothing particularly new, much like the concept of intelligent machines and advanced A.I. themselves. By 1965, British cryptologist and mathematician Irving J. Good had begun using the expression *intelligence explosion,* which specifically entails a rapid increase in technological innovation, following the emergence of either some form of A.I., or of brain-computer interfaces that would allow the human mind to exceed natural levels of intelligence. Thus, a positive feedback loop would be created, in which the growth rate of technology, now in the hands of intelligence that surpasses natural human abilities, would literally seem to "explode." The modern use of the term *Singularity* in reference to such an intelligence explosion came much later in 1983; mathematician and science fiction writer Vernor Vinge coined the term by likening the result of an intelligence explosion to standard models of physics breaking down in midst of observing the event horizon of a black hole:

> We will soon create intelligences greater than our own. When this happens, human history will have reached a kind of singularity, an intellectual transition as impenetrable as the knotted space-time at the center of a black hole, and the world will pass far beyond our understanding.[15]

Ideas pertaining to nuclear war or some other pending disaster were common themes amidst Vinge's interpretations of a future intelligence explosion. Paired alongside his first specific mention of *technological Singularity* in a print publication, Vinge had noted:

> Barring a worldwide catastrophe, I believe that technology will achieve our wildest dreams, and soon. When we raise our own intelligence and that of our creations, we are no longer in a world of human-sized characters. At that point we have fallen into a technological "black hole," a technological singularity.[16]

Sentiments of pending disaster similar to those Vinge expressed had appeared a few years earlier in the work of ufologist Jacques Vallee, who, by the late 1970s, had expounded on ideas quite relevant to a technological Singularity in a handful of scientific journals. Specifically, this culminated in an essay he coauthored with Professor Francois Meyer that appeared in the journal *Technological Forecasting and Social Change* in 1975, titled "The Dynamics of Long-Term Growth." Though the term *Singularity* was never used specifically, Vallee and Meyer discussed an observable trend where technology appears to grow rapidly enough to exceed mere exponential growth, instead representing a greater-than-exponential hyperbolic rate. Eventually, the rate of technological growth, paired with the expansion of population the world over, would reach a similar point of "Singularity," beyond which the predictable outcomes would become difficult to determine. "The forecast of infinite growth in a finite time interval is absurd," the authors write. "All we can expect of these developments is that some damping effect will take place very soon. The only question is whether this will be accomplished through 'soft regulation' or catastrophe."[17] We might note here, of course, that such perceptions of eventual demise likely reflected the cultural sentiments of the day—namely fears of mutually assured destruction that had been rife throughout the Cold War era.

That said, although the ideas and attitudes leading up to the formalization of the Singularity concept were many and varied indeed, today there are much more distinct views held among futurists and proponents of an intelligence explosion lingering in our future. According to the Singularity Institute, which defines Singularity as being simply "the technological creation of smarter-than-human intelligence,"[18] there are much broader implications native to the concept that evoke questions about how we will define intelligence in the coming years. For instance, will it matter if a conscious entity is a living biological being, rather than merely an intelligent machine, when it comes to major decisions that will take place in future societies? Furthermore, when it comes to distinctions between biology and machines, will there even be any discernible difference once A.I. reaches a point that it cannot only replicate itself, but might also *improve* its "offspring"? Indeed, such a future technology may effectively blur any existing distinctions between man and machine, perhaps allowing the focus to shift solely toward the unobstructed pursuit of technological growth—and despite whatever intelligence may ultimately come to exist behind it. This concept, as outlined in an overview provided on the Website of the Singularity Institute, supposes that A.I. would be best suited for initiating such a trend, though it also surmises that biologically augmented humans would be capable of the same:

> Smarter minds will be more effective at building still smarter minds. This loop appears most clearly in the example of an Artificial Intelligence improving its own source code, but it would also arise...from

humans with direct brain-computer interfaces creating the next generation of brain-computer interfaces, or biologically augmented humans working on an Artificial Intelligence project.[19]

Given the scenario previously outlined, our concept of an "intelligence explosion" is thus realized. But additionally, perhaps notions of "biologically augmented humans" and A.I. capable of "improving itself" presented here also begin to evoke stirrings in the minds of those familiar with UFO literature. Arguably, among various theories pertaining to UFO origins, ideas such as visitors from the future—as well as the more popular notion of aliens from other planets—could both easily incorporate futuristic post-Singularity concepts into attempts at drawing likely explanations.

For instance, the presence of nanotechnological wonders like J. Storrs Hall's *foglets*, which are described as swarms of miniature devices working in tandem that represent "one conceptual design for creating real morphable bodies,"[20] might easily be used in attempts to explain the behavior of supposed alien beings. In Ray Fowler's *The Andreasson Affair*, abductee Betty Andreasson describes how extraterrestrial visitors had entered her home by literally passing through a closed wooden door, moving "in a jerky motion, leaving a vapory image behind."[21] Armed with the predicted issuance of something similar to foglet-technology, we might go so far as to suppose that some artificial intelligence comprised of a moldable swarm of nanobots would be capable of passing through physical objects in this way, thus engaging in self-reassembly after breaking apart for purposes of moving through something like a wooden door.

However, especially within the scope of our present discussion, an anthropocentric approach becomes far too easy with our examination of how future technology will lead to things that are quite "alien" by our scientific and cultural standards today. Indeed, nanotechnology, in addition to the incredible possibilities afforded to us by brain-computer interfaces or advanced A.I., are less often projected beyond their expected physical augmentations of the human body. This, of course, applies well to the discussion of presumed alien life forms, as described throughout the accounts of UFO abductees. However, when we consider the behavior of the actual UFO aircraft, based on eyewitness descriptions, there are indeed a number of elements that are equally strange by nature— if not seemingly impossible—but that also bear some similarity to the forecasts of our futurists today. Rather than speeding off into the stars at tremendous speeds and disappearing into space, UFOs just as often seem to simply disappear, *period.* As Vallee and many others have observed already, they will often tend to vanish outright, or will sometimes seem to begin entering or merging with the *ground* when making their exit—whatever is really necessary, perhaps, so long as they are removed from the view of humans who may be observing nearby.

And yet, the sheer number of reports, and perhaps more importantly, the hypothetical number of presumed UFO landings based on computer models, would have their appearances far outranking the numbers expected, for instance, with regard to an alien survey of planet Earth. In his book *Dimensions,* Jacques Vallee writes, "[T]aking a conservative multiplying factor often leads us to the staggering conclusion that the UFOs...must have landed here no fewer than *three million times* in two decades!"[22] This is indeed a tremendous number of landings, and one that far exceeds the amount of time spent on Earth needed for mere completion of a survey of this planet (though again, here we are judging the intentions of UFO occupants according to our own understanding of science, cultural values, and so forth). Nonetheless, such deviations from the anticipated models of space exploration have led Vallee, along with a few others throughout the years, to propose notions so bold as the literal staging of UFO appearances by whatever intelligence may represent them:

> This is one of the little recognized facts of the UFO problem that any theory has yet to explain. The theory of random visitation does *not* explain it. Either the UFOs select their witnesses for psychological or sociological reasons, or they are something entirely different from space vehicles. In either case, their appearances are *staged!*[23]

This is certainly a possibility, though there would need to be a hefty reason for using technology so advanced as that displayed by UFO craft for mere purposes of staging psychological experiments with humans. Granted, Vallee's interpretation here was not intended entirely as justification for any sort of "staging" along these lines. Instead, his hope was to draw attention to the bigger question: What could possibly allow these UFOs to have such prolific interaction with Earth and its inhabitants, *especially* if the intelligence behind them were extraterrestrial? Furthermore, does this warrant our consideration of other explanations, especially those that are terrestrial in nature? Could we stand a better chance in terms of accounting for the inconsistencies present within UFO literature if we begin to divorce ourselves from the old notion that flying saucers and similar aircraft are the *obvious* work of aliens from outer space? What about an interdimensional intelligence, whose presence is betrayed by physical anomalies that become apparent in our skies? Might indigenous *cryptoterrestrials,* to borrow the convention of the late author Mac Tonnies, be a factor worthy of consideration here? And yes, might we stand to gain anything from exploring notions of *temporal displacement,* in the event that some future intelligence has harnessed an ability to move across points in time as simply as you or I might stroll through an outdoor garden?

Artificial intelligence, advanced bioengineering, anti-gravitational aircraft, and perhaps even time travel are all things that could account for various UFO technologies. However, each of these possibilities is equally fastened to the idea of a coming technological Singularity just as well. It is time now that we begin to cross-examine these mutual potentials and see where the *real* similarities may indeed lay. The results of our present foray will no doubt amaze us, and at times may even be troubling. But perhaps most importantly, they will serve in helping us better understand the technology underlying these mysterious and enigmatic UFOs, as well as their

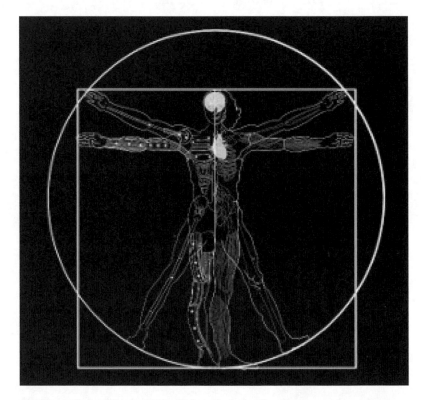

"Man of the Year 2112" by Caleb Hanks.

curiously reticent occupants. For all we know, our perception of supposed extraterrestrial technologies may one day
reach a point of convergence, where those things "alien"
to us now will unite with our expectations for life on Earth
in some distant epoch. Perhaps by the year 2112, in addition to no virtual distinctions remaining between man and
machine, there will be just as few that exist to separate
what we call *human* and *alien*.

Chapter 2

Assembling an Anomaly:
The Collation of Future Science and Alien Technology

*The false but widespread assumption that
a UFO is, of necessity, an alien spaceship
is usually the reason the term generates
such an exaggerated and confusing range
of emotional responses. A recognition of
the extraterrestrial hypothesis as being
a valid, although unproved, possible
explanation worthy of further scientific
scrutiny is something entirely different
from approaching the subject of UFOs as if
this discovery had already been made.*

— Leslie Kean,
*UFOs: Generals, Pilots, and Government
Officials Go on the Record*

Since my early youth, I admit to being wholly absorbed with all the compelling possibilities that surrounded the UFO mystery. Even the grainiest and least aesthetically impressive black and white photographs that had emerged into the wide and ever-expanding dossier of UFO reports up to that time boasted a certain degree of promise in my young mind. To me, each of those otherwise-unimpressive images, depicting amorphous globs of light and barely discernible shapes coasting through the airspace above our planet, might have held the potential for incredible realities and bold new kinds of life that might have come from, of all places, somewhere outside this little celestial island we call Earth.

It is rather strange to me now, thinking back to those years of eager and hopeful early exploits in the field of ufology, that notions regarding the origins of those strange saucers—at least so far as being from someplace other than outer space—had seldom crossed my mind. Today, things are quite different, and I can state with certainty that the man I would eventually become, equipped with a more complete understanding of the scientific methodology that any serious researcher must apply in his or her respective field, has illuminated a number of new potentials in the realm of what UFOs might be. If anything, my thought processes regarding the possibilities this complicated mystery may yet afford us have only continued to broaden, especially the further I get from that old notion that UFOs, quite simply, are interstellar spacecraft from another world.

To be fair, the reasoned scientist should not (nor would he in practice) eliminate *any* possibility on the mere grounds that available evidence seemed to be lacking in one particular area or another. For all we know of the UFOs themselves—or the *presumption* that they are occupied by some kind of physical beings like you or me, for that matter—the ongoing enigma of the flying saucers very well may be representative of alien life from some distant star system. Therefore, far be it from me, let alone the staunchest skeptics among us, to hope to derail anyone else's belief in alien visitation here on Earth. The bottom line is that *we simply don't know what, exactly, we may be dealing with when it comes to UFOs.* At present, we only have a few reasonably good ideas.

Based on this fundamental notion that UFOs could either be *nothing* we have yet imagined, or that they are represented by a variety of different unexplained aerial phenomena, I have long advocated the use of a reasoned, philosophical process of inquiry we might call "speculative ufology" for use in their study. Although many in the scientific field lapse into a state of rhetorical cringes and curls at the mere utterance of that word—*speculation*—there must be some way to proceed with the unraveling of complex mysteries through the use of filling in certain blank areas, so as to ponder a more likely outcome or resolution to any given set of circumstances. Think for a moment of how a skilled mathematician or physicist is given license, by virtue of his trade, to balance equations that are intricate in their difficulty by brainstorming a host of different *variables*. That is, he will go about the problem-solving process by replacing certain unknown elements with quantities that may, in the end, bring resolution to a group of numbers arranged in such a way that they represent the complex mysteries surrounding things like time, space, gravity, and the cosmos. At the outset of his inquiry, this brilliant man of science will likely not be equipped with every piece needed to solve the puzzle before him; and thus, he *improvises*. This sort of educated guesswork is integral to the eventual unraveling of any great and complex mystery our universe may have to offer.

Much the same as math and numbers can be likened to being a universal language of the greater cosmos, the role of the *speculative physicist* is one who seeks to find "common ground" between disparate elements that exist throughout our reality. Why is it, for instance, that light energy in the form of photons being propelled through space will tend to behave differently in some parts of the universe as opposed to others? Though there may appear to be no physical mass present to influence their behavior, the light traveling along in such circumstances can be observed behaving as though there were, in fact, something else there. Hence, such strange and questionable behavior has lead us to the presumption that things like black holes and antimatter must exist, and that the latter of these will likely share the same attractant forces that any "normal" matter would exert in terms of its influence on other objects. This, at least, has become a consensus among many in the scientific community, so far as being the most likely explanation for weird behavior that can be seen out there in deep space, and at times, perhaps even in our own backyard. The great challenge, however (or burden, depending on one's viewpoint), always lies in the task of confirming such theories, a task that inevitably becomes daunting.

We are cursed with a very limited ability to physically lay our hands on such mysteries as antimatter—and the same goes for things we would perceive as being normal and everyday, such as light energy. We are unable to hold such things in our hands, turning them before our eyes and grasping them like any solid object, in order to observe their most miniscule and clandestine details. But because of this, can we say with certainty that light energy simply does not exist? Can we say that antimatter, despite its elusive nature, is not what we had originally presumed must be exerting its peculiar influences on other aspects of our universe? The modern scientist would scoff at the very proposition, right? And yet, that seems to be *precisely* how complex issues involving the UFO mystery end up being treated.

So why is there such a double standard here? How can bizarre concepts like alternate dimensions and time travel be completely acceptable, but only as long as there is a speculative physicist with a long string of letters after his name who divulges such potentials—and often standing before a camera's ever-watchful eye, presenting these bold "theories" to an audience of millions in some colorful science-themed television program? As soon as the humble ufologist steps up to the plate and begins to point out the scientific potentials that may surround things like UFO propulsion, or how intelligent life might travel through space, he gets laughed off the stage and called a lunatic. *Go back home, freak. And try fitting that tin foil hat a bit tighter next time; you're going to need it to protect your brain from being fried by those aliens you spend all day thinking about.*

Yet unlike antimatter, there have been a number of photographs, videos, and reliable eyewitness testimonies that have emerged throughout the years that illustrate quite clearly how an entire host of intelligently controlled objects have been observed, albeit at sparring intervals, soaring through our skies. And to wit, as addressed earlier, these objects have succeeded in garnering attention from intelligence agencies in the United States and elsewhere around the world time and time again. Despite the physical, observable nature of this phenomenon, the bottom line continues to be that, despite any amount of evidence promoting their existence, in large part the scientific community still seems to feel that *there is little or no scientific merit to continuing UFO studies.* After all, what could we possibly learn from the *speculative* study of things that appear so advanced that we can barely fathom what greater meaning or relevance they may keep for us as a species?

At this time, I suggest we put forth a new, different kind of bold idea: I say to hell with this "holier than thou" attitude toward the act of speculation, which we see so rife amid the greater scientific mainstream. Had Einstein or Oppenheimer never engaged in *reasoned* speculation, allowing their imaginations to drift away at times on the mere hope of possibility, then the proponents of things such as antimatter and alternate dimensions might instead find themselves employed among the ranks of one of your neighborhood fast food chains. Let's give credit to some of our very finest speculators where credit is due.

Rather than to place limitations on thought and shy away from reasoned speculation, if we are to take on a greater, more complete understanding of what we call the UFO mystery, we must press on, pushing ahead by asking questions. Occasionally, we must fit variables into the gaps and spaces we uncover, fitting carefully molded ideas into the nooks and crannies of logic much like the steady hand of the mathematician, as he draws lines and symbols upon the powdery surface of his chalkboard. Above all, we must use this logic and reason we obtain to discern what we can from what sparring evidence we have been afforded at this time.

Remembering the words of Spock, Captain Kirk's unexcitable science advisor aboard the Starship *Enterprise* in J.J. Abrams's 2009 re-visioning of the *Star Trek* mythos: "Once you have eliminated the impossible, whatever remains, however improbable, must be the truth." The same quote can, in fact, be traced to a much earlier source: none other than Sir Arthur Conan Doyle's famous sleuth, Sherlock Holmes. Regardless of the origin of the phrase, I'm certain neither character—Spock nor Holmes—would disapprove of the logic I'm advocating here.

Although UFOs had certainly managed to capture my fascination as a youth, I cannot claim to have seen the same appeal in many of the other things children my age were interested in. Whereas I think every young boy will go through a phase of thinking robots are extremely awesome with their mechanical workings and, as seen often in books and film, apparent shape-shifting abilities, characters like Optimus Prime and the popular *Transformers* cartoons had never quite succeeded in grabbing my attention. Instead, my enjoyment of the Autobots and their exploits would come much later, only after seeing the more recent film renditions directed by Michael Bay. In the films, a remarkably dramatic representation of the classic Hasbro figures and their morphing abilities was afforded to us as viewers, woven around a storyline that cast Earth as the battleground for an ongoing struggle between two warring factions: Optimus Prime and his noble Autobot kindred, and the evil and destructive Decepticons.

Although the Transformers might best represent any young boy's hope for gratuitous robotic violence and destruction at its finest, they also present us with a unique circumstance worthy of further consideration: Optimus Prime and his fellow Transformers aren't biological life forms, but are instead intelligent, conscious entities that are able to change their physical shape and structure at will because they are mechanized, artificial beings. In short, the Transformers represent *advanced artificial intelligence from another world.*

The notion that human interaction with non-terrestrial intelligences that might be artificial by design, rather than biological in nature, presents a number of unique considerations, many of which we will explore in greater depth later in this book. For the time being, our allusion to *Transformers* serves as a unique springboard, propelling us further toward our foray into attempts at better understanding the ways humans might one day intermingle with varieties of intelligence that exceed our own. In truth, this sort of interaction may already be occurring, though without arming ourselves with the proper cultural and technological frames of reference needed to recognize them, we may not even be able to perceive such interactions at present. Think, for instance, of the anthill situated mere inches from the shoulder of a busy roadway. With every passing vehicle, the busy workers and drones must feel an Earth-shaking rumble within their subterranean community, as they perform diligently for their queen. Few, however, would ever stop to consider the cause of the great tremors that might occasionally shake dust from the ceilings of their tunnels and burrows. Arguably, the sudden realization that there were enormous, intelligent beings only a few feet away would become a horrifying prospect for the lowly worker ant.

Then again, if humans were ever to learn that there were enormous, intelligent beings only a few feet away from us, occasionally pondering our existence—or maybe even our apparent *insignificance*—wouldn't we be equally terrified by this unusual prospect?

This sort of analogy has been utilized before by the likes of Michio Kaku and a number of others, with attempts at reconciling the notion that human perception, much like that of the ant, may be very limited at times. Though we can conceptualize the ideas surrounding intelligent life like ourselves existing elsewhere in the universe, many of us nonetheless ridicule and poke fun at the idea of alien visitation as described in gross detail by the purported alien abductee. One may find this truism particularly interesting to note, especially after a careful examination of the work that is best known among all the alien abductees, Whitley Strieber, who shows that his own views regarding interactions he had with so-called "visitors" had not entailed the perception that they were necessarily extraterrestrial at the outset. In fact, his earliest suppositions involved a very terrestrial scenario, where his captors could have emerged, albeit covertly, from someplace right here in our midst:

> It could be that the "visitors" were really from here. Certainly the long tradition of fairy lore suggested that something had been with us for far more than the forty or fifty years since the phenomenon took on its present appearance. The only trouble with this theory was that what has been happening since

the mid-forties seemed more than just a little different from the fairy lore. Now there were brain probes and flying disks involved, abductions and grey creatures with staring eyes.... Another thought was that the visitors might really be our own dead. Maybe we were a larval form, and the adults of our species were as incomprehensible to us, as totally unimaginable, as the butterfly must be to the caterpillar. Perhaps the dead had been having their own technological revolution, and were learning to break through the limits of their bourne.

Or perhaps something very real had emerged from our own unconscious mind...coming forth to haunt us. Maybe belief creates its own reality. It could be that the gods of the past were strong because the belief of their followers actually *did* give them life, and maybe that was happening again. We were creating drab, postindustrial gods in place of the glorious beings of the past. Instead of Apollo riding his fiery chariot across the sky or the goddess of night spreading her cloak of stars, we had created little steel-gray gods with the souls of pirates and craft no more beautiful inside than the bilges of battleships.[1]

Despite one's own feelings regarding Strieber and his claims, credit must be awarded not only on account of his artful prose, but also for his ability to reasonably contemplate the various potentials surrounding him at the outset of his ongoing "transformation." Fascinating though his ideas and ponderings were up to this point, he then goes one step further, and puts forth something that, with direct relevance to our present discussion, is quite novel indeed:

> Or maybe we were receiving a visit from another dimension, or even from another time. Maybe what we were seeing were human time travelers who assumed the disguise of extraterrestrial visitors in order to avoid creating some sort of catastrophic temporal paradox by revealing their presence to their own ancestors.[2]

Visitors from our future, he asks? Could such a thing even be possible, when considering all the other sorts of factors surrounding the UFO mystery? Perhaps, to be fair, this futuristic hypothesis is really as solid as any other, when weighing the multitude of potentials before us. And yet, despite the promise that emerges with it at conception, the burden of providing some kind of empirical evidence for visitors from our future—or virtually any other idea in the realm of the evasive and elusive UFO—seems next to impossible.

In *Communion*, Strieber highlights several of the immediate problems with the "time traveler" premise for us right at the outset. He supposes, for instance, that there could be some element of deception at play beneath what was apparently meant to appear to be some sort of abduction experience. Engaging in a thought experiment where his kidnappers might have donned an extraterrestrial disguise, Strieber then suggests that they could have done so in order to protect against "some sort of catastrophic temporal paradox," as outlined in the previous excerpt. But would an element of careful deception even this elaborate really allay the sorts of "temporal paradoxes" that Strieber supposed might emerge? In other words, could hiding behind the façade of an alien presence do enough to prevent the potentially harmful tampering of a future humanity, whose attempts at engaging with their past might yield destructive side effects in the chronology of human history?

Aiming to rectify the potential disasters associated with hypothetical "grandfather paradoxes," where human travel backward in time could alter the future in danger-ous ways, scientists have again found themselves caving to the damnable temptation of speculation. Even with no proof yet that time travel does or does not exist, the phil-osophical debate alone that has erupted around how it may be achieved has led to the creation of a host of remarkable new scientific theories. Arguably, one of the most popu-lar among these incorporates parallel universes into the equation. Israeli-British physicist David Deutsch of Oxford University's Mathematical Institute has argued since the early 1990s that if one were to succeed at developing a process in which reverse time travel were indeed possible, the hypothetical time traveler would likely end up in an entirely different "branch" of history, altogether separate from that which he arrived. This would mean that, rather than a single, linear plane of existence that constitutes time, there may be a number of alternate dimensions that result from the various possible outcomes of any given

situation. Each of these dimensions could follow very different courses, based solely on factors like chance and
probability related with any set of circumstances that may
transpire someplace in the universe. The resulting scientific theories formulated around such ideas have led to
popular notions such as a *superstring theory* of alternate
parallel dimensions, as well as a subsequent "M-theory"
designed to unite the many problems associated with various string theories where only 10 hypothetical dimensions
may exist.[3]

Although alternate parallel dimensions obviously
become useful in one's effort to justify the paradoxes of
time travel, one important thing that must be remembered
is that dimensional theories of parallel existence and other
ideas involving the less-easily reconciled aspects of space
and time *are still only theories.* No matter how well jus-
tified they may seem, or from whom their advocacy may
arrive, we cannot accept speculation as pure fact simply
on the good faith that our talking heads on prime-time
television would not mislead us. All too often, people are
willing to sit down and watch their favorite network television programs that appear to be dissecting the deeper
aspects of our existence—whether those programs pur-
port to deal with subjects like alternate dimensions, or
even UFOs and extraterrestrial visitors in ancient times—
and they accept these things entirely as facts. We tend to
forget that virtually anything seen on television, however
credible it may appear to be, has been bestowed with a

greater priority that supersedes the merit of presenting factual information—and this priority demands that what appears must first be *entertaining*, above all else. Only then, so long as the content first offers interesting and compelling information that viewers will want to watch, will the facts be allowed to trickle down.

While this sort of prioritization of compelling content placed over factual merit may not be causing any real harm to anybody, it has certainly been effective in skewing people's beliefs and attitudes when it comes to the complexities associated with the nature of reality and our universe. And this is certainly not intended to mean that nothing we see or hear on television can be trusted—only that once we understand the levels of prioritization that influence what we hear, and how we hear it, we would be wise to take virtually *anything* we hear with a grain of salt, and a healthy ounce or two of skepticism.

All this kept in mind, perhaps we should also consider whether the extra-dimensional qualities popularly associated with space-time, although meeting the criteria for being potential realities (and *very* compelling television content), could also be unnecessary as tools for explaining aspects of the hidden universe around us. Perhaps, based on the limitations of human perception, and the resulting philosophical concepts that emerge—for which we assign such names as "space" or "time"—the grand illusion that constitutes our reality really does have us fooled. The reality we perceive as a chronological progression through past, present, and future may in fact be as illusory as the mirage that haunts the thirsty eyes of some lost and weary traveler. The oasis he seeks, which he will no doubt become convinced he can see in the distance, is the partial result of physical properties of nature misleading him, paired with a sincere desire on his own part to see that oasis in the first place.

It may be that, although technological achievements from our future *are* actually capable of influencing what we perceive as being events taking place in our present day, this may not require physical travel through "time" at all, let alone the existence of alternate dimensions. Furthermore, if we could suppose that time as we know it, represented by our own chronological progression through history, were an artifact of human perception, who is to say that humans of the future would need to be capable of "traveling" through time in order to perceive past, present, and future as a single, conjoined entity? To a future civilization whose levels of perception greatly exceed yours or mine, perhaps through the aid of cybernetic enhancements and other innovative science that await us in the coming years, moving through what we perceive as "time" could become a very different process—and far more easy.

And to be fair, there certainly are empirical studies that demonstrate how time is not the unbendable constant that we typically perceive. For instance, we are aware of the effects of what is called time dilation, which constitutes a difference between the way time passes relative to different gravitational masses, or even two individuals traveling relative to each other. While this concept has become a fundamental precept within the physics theory of relativity, it illustrates with surprising finesse how time is not really everything we make it out to be.

Imagine a clock sitting on the ground that has been synchronized perfectly with an identical clock sitting nearby. A man arrives with his wife, and while he sits and watches one of the clocks, his wife takes the other with her on an airplane, which travels high into the sky, and at great speed. In this instance, differences between the passage of time relative to the two clocks becomes measurable; this is because the effects of a single source of gravity exerted against two objects can vary, based on such things as the distance each object is from that initial source of gravity, as well as the speed they may be traveling. And to be precise, what, exactly, is being affected is *the passage of time itself,* relative to either of those two objects and the conditions surrounding them.

The same general experiment just outlined has taken place more than once, each time displaying predictable outcomes based on relativity theory.[4] This presents for us the notion that there are likely to be a number of odd universal conditions that, as we've begun to see already, humans are largely incapable of perceiving directly. For instance, because the effects of gravity on the passage of time differ in relation to the distance from the object exerting a gravitational force, when we walk down the street each day, our head and shoulders are literally passing through time at a slightly different rate from that which our feet are traveling, because the latter are closer to the Earth and hence influenced differently by its gravitational pull. Though this is strange indeed, the effects are so minute that they are imperceptible to people going about their daily lives, and thus are very seldom even considered. We have adapted with time to function within these conditions, and with little thought about the actual mechanisms that may be underlying such simple acts as an afternoon stroll.

To be clear, the reason we illustrate all this here is because experiments with time dilation, with respect to their repeatable effects, show us that what we perceive as time is indeed somewhat pliable, and that physical actions humans may take can indeed cause minor shifts in the way time passes around us. We are still a long way from being able to harness any degree of functional manipulation of time, but we are nonetheless made aware, at least, of such realistic potentials. To apply this practically, especially with regard to the effects of time in relation to advanced UFO aircraft, Nigel Calder illustrates in his book *Magic Universe: A Grand Tour of Modern Science* how physical travel through space at tremendous speed might even constitute a form of time travel in itself:

> If you want to exploit special relativity to keep you alive for as long as possible, the most comfortable way to travel through the Universe will be to accelerate steadily at 1*g*—the rate at which objects fall under gravity at the Earth's surface. Then you will have no problems with weightlessness, and you can

in theory make amazing journeys during a human lifetime. This is because the persistent acceleration will take you to within a whisker of the speed of light.

Your body-clock will come almost to a standstill compared with the passage of time on Earth and on passing stars. Through your window you will see stars rushing toward you, and not only because of the direct effect of your motion toward them. The apparent distance that you have to go keeps shrinking, as another effect of relativity at high speeds.

In a 1g spaceship, you can set out at age 20 for example, and travel right out if our Galaxy to the Andromeda Galaxy, which is 2 million light-years away. By starting in good time to slow down (still at 1g), you can land on a planet in the next galaxy and celebrate your 50th birthday there. Have a look around before setting off for home, and you can still be back for your 80th birthday. But who knows what state you'll find the Earth to be in, millions of years from now? [5]

One thing that could be implied here, with direct relevance to there being some potential connection between UFOs and time travel, involves the intricate interrelationship between high-speed travel through space, which UFOs are often observed doing, and the effects of time dilation and other conditions on the presumed occupants of such craft. Perhaps UFOs would not necessarily have to represent the exploits of "time travelers" from Earth's own future, at least in the literal sense, for a connection to exist in this regard. The effects of time dilation, and perhaps even the intentional, controlled manipulation of space-time itself, might come into play with any aircraft capable of technology that would allow the high-speed maneuverability often described in certain more incredible UFO reports. Thus, if we consider whether space-time might consist of certain illusory elements, often capable of misleading our incomplete human perception of reality around us, we might also have an easier time accepting that certain aspects of the greater UFO mystery, as Streiber and others have supposed already, could be related somehow with technology emanating from our own future. Still, while the notion presents an intriguing possibility, it must remain merely food for thought, for now at least.

Understanding how this interaction may be taking place and, perhaps more importantly, grounding ourselves in such a way that will allow us to better predict where future technologies may arise that will shed some potential light on this mystery, are far easier said than done. Therefore, in order to understand the vast potentials for an existent future technology that may await us, a surprising amount of knowledge may be gained from looking to our past; this is especially the case when we consider the years immediately following the Second World War, in which the obvious presence of some kind of incredible—and potentially dangerous—new technology appeared in our midst, which were dubbed "flying saucers." Indeed, the more obvious instances of early UFO encounters date back to the mid- and late 1940s. However, our examination of the potential for highly advanced, post-Singularity technologies in our midst (regardless of their specific origin, whether that be extraterrestrial or something else) will inevitably take us even further back in time—more than a century, in fact—to an era when the evidence for a variety of unique, advanced, and intelligently controlled technologies may have already begun to surface here on Earth.

Chapter 3

Divergent Potentials:

Mysterious New Technology

*In one's frustration it is all too easy to
seize on an explanation of the "Men from
Mars" variety and to ignore the many
UFO features unaccounted for.... We may
be inadvertently and artificially increasing
the significance of the conspicuous features
while the part we ignore—or that which
is not reported by the untrained witness—
may contain the clue to the whole subject.*
                              —Dr. J. Allen Hynek,
              The UFO Experience: A Scientific Enquiry

The year was 1889, and a sudden frenzy had erupted among the members of a respected Philadelphia-area flight enthusiasts' group known as the Weldon Institute. There, in the midst of the respectable assembly, a stranger had appeared—or rather, had *intruded*—whose imposing physical stature "was a regular trapezium with the greatest of its parallel sides formed by the line of his shoulders."[1] The man had willingly cast himself as a pariah on the afternoon in question, after boldly claiming in midst of the world's greatest proponents of dirigible aircraft not only that the future of aviation lay in the use of heavier-than-air flying machines, but that he had already mastered the skies with this very sort of device.

"As man has become master of the seas with the ship, by the oar, the sail, the wheel and the screw, so shall he become master of atmospherical space by apparatus heavier than the air," the infidel proclaimed to the angry congregation before him. "For it must be heavier to be stronger than the air!"[2]

Blasphemy, they thought, just as the members of the Weldon Institute spilled into the hallway, chasing this irreverent bastard and his trifling ideas from the room before he further befouled the sanctity of their gentlemen's lodge. And then, as abruptly as he had managed to enter their secluded little world, this man seemingly *vanished* right in their midst—or so it had appeared. While the bewildered members of the Weldon Institute conversed excitedly with one another about this upset, their strange guest had been whisked into the air above, spirited away into the open sky by an enigmatic new flying technology he alone had managed to innovate.

Of course, the observant reader may already be aware that the dramatic portrayal of events unfolding were not recovered from the minutes of any real aviation club's proceedings, nor was this man Robur, the dissident in question, ever the captain of any real heavier-than-air flying vehicle that had already managed to conquer the skies by 1889. The only real truth behind these events is that they appeared in print for the first time in 1886 under the title *Robur-le-Conquérant,* having been translated later into the English language and released to American audiences as a novel called *The Clipper of the Clouds* and, more popularly, *Robur the Conqueror.*[3]

Robur's indignant approach to staking his claim on the open air, as envisaged by science fiction author Jules Verne, may have seemed like utter fantasy to most readers, and even Verne himself, who masterfully was able to pen accounts of people and places in countries he had never once visited. And yet, the enigma of Robur, so-called "Master of the World," and, of course, his unusual flying vessel, may have been far closer to reality than Verne himself, or many of his readers, had ever realized.

The entire episode really began to coalesce with a well-known series of events that took place on the evening of Tuesday, November 17, 1896, in the skies over Sacramento, California. Just after eight o'clock a bright light was seen traveling through the sky, initially making no noise, as it appeared over the eastern horizon. The craft had been traveling slowly, occasionally bobbing up and down or from side to side as it glided overhead, which, in retrospect, seems reminiscent of descriptions quite familiar to modern UFO researchers that involve the so-called "falling leaf" pattern of descent, resembling a leaf gliding back and forth on its way to the ground.[4] Among those who were said to have witnessed the strange apparition drifting through Sacramento's night skies that evening had been the assistant to California's secretary of state, as well as the daughter of the town mayor. Later reports would continue in the days that followed, with sightings reported by members of the mayor's staff, as well as the Sacramento-area district attorney and deputy sheriff.[5]

Scads of similar reports would ensue after the strange lights were witnessed above Sacramento, and soon an entire "airship scare" was underway, with reports of similar objects coming in from other parts of the country. According to some witnesses, the large white light drifting silently through the sky had been only one part of the strange object in question; some accounts divulged that a larger apparatus existed that the light had been attached to, variously resembling a huge egg or having an oblong shape similar to a cigar. Some of the more imaginative descriptions included fanciful descriptions of rudders, paddle wheels, or even propellers helping to keep the massive floating fortress aloft, becoming starkly reminiscent of Verne's depiction of a heavier than air warship in *Robur the Conqueror*.

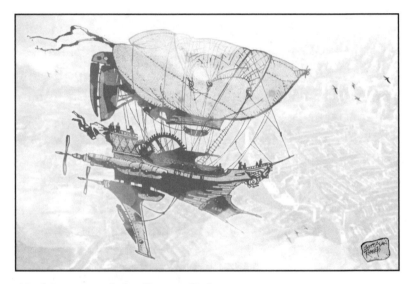

Airship artwork by Scotty Roberts.

Such stories of "phantom airships" seen throughout the United States during the late 1890s are largely taken tongue in cheek, and are considered among the better examples of newspaper hoaxes that were common among the various daily newspapers throughout the late 19th century. And yet, though many of the stories lumped in alongside the phantom airship reports are obviously the pure imaginings of clever (or bored) newspapermen of the day, there are a few aspects to the mystery that remain worthy of consideration. For one, the more credible sightings—especially those from the Sacramento area in November of 1896—generally seem to describe what could be likened to some kind of dirigible craft, though perhaps with certain capabilities that may have been capable of outperforming various known airships of the day. Second, the veracity of some of these reports could, arguably, rest more soundly on the groupings of individuals who had claimed to see the strange object over Sacramento. As stated, these seemed to include city officials and a number of other respectable members of the community. In other words, some would argue that it not only seems likely that something *was* seen over Southern California and surrounding areas in the late autumn of 1896, but also that it is far from impossible for certain technologies to have existed around the time, which would be needed to produce an aircraft similar to those described in the "phantom airship" reports.

One of the best presentations on this subject in the available literature is J. Allen Danelek's *The Great Airship of 1897*. Danelek's book, although highly speculative in its presentation, discusses the possibility that some private entity—perhaps an individual funded by wealthy investment dollars stemming from somewhere in Southern California—could have built an exotic-looking aircraft that, while utilizing comparatively primitive technology available just before the turn of the last century, nonetheless outperformed other known aircraft of the day. Hoping to protect the obvious potential for profiting from such technology (especially once it became a feasible option to go public with the design and incorporate commercial enterprises thereafter), the craft, along with the clandestine sources behind its creation and funding, might have been kept largely a secret from the public. Then, by April 1897, very little was heard anymore regarding the blimp-like mystery airships, which Danelek supposes could indicate the onset of some kind of disaster; perhaps the vessel crashed or was destroyed in some other way.[6]

Interestingly, the United States wasn't the only country in which reports of strange "mystery airships" would begin to occur quite early, especially with relation to the kinds of technology apparently being used. Little more than a decade after the strange aircraft first seen over Sacramento made its rather curious presence known, similar reports then began to emanate from Australia that involved bright, colored lights seen in the skies. According to an August 9, 1909, story that appeared in *The Barrier Miner*:

> The Rev. B. Cozens, of the Port Melbourne Seamen's Mission, tells an interesting story regarding the mysterious lights which appeared in the air over the Dandenong Ranges on Saturday night. Going outside at 10 o'clock, he saw, half a mile up in the air, two revolving lights moving over

the ranges. They slowed down, dipped, and rose up again, then changed from white to red and to blue. Mr. Cozens called his wife and three neighbours. They all watched the lights until midnight, by which time one had almost moved out of sight over the ranges. Again at 2 o'clock Mr. Cozens saw the second one, which almost crossed the ranges. Five more appeared in the distance, moving in the direction taken by the other two.[7]

Australian researcher Andrew Nicholson brought this report, along with several others from around the same time, to my attention, noting that: "Passengers on the Melbourne express also witnessed the light, which had been seen the previous two nights flying above the Southern Highlands and the coast between Mittagong and Wollongong."[8] According to an article in the *Sydney Morning Herald* that described the event, it was believed that the witnesses had probably seen "a balloon or airship."[9]

Many point out that, although approaches by those like Danelek are indeed speculative endeavors (and to be clear, the author himself states this early on in his book), the thesis Danelek presents does illustrate a few important elements worthy of consideration. Because the technology needed to produce the craft described in various eyewitness reports could easily have existed by 1896, the case could also be made that the craft being seen around the time would hardly fit the conventional "extraterrestrial" model of what many take UFOs to be. In fact, Danelek's own feelings seem to be quite the contrary:

What I found most curious about the whole affair—
and a point which I believe has been overlooked
by most commentators over the years—is that at
the time, most witnesses thought the vehicle was
neither imaginary nor extraterrestrial. Instead,
most believed it to have been a very man-made
machine—a powered balloon perhaps or, more
accurately, a dirigible—being tested in the chilly
night air of North America. In other words, they
saw it as neither hoax nor alien visitor, but simply as an example of nascent technology being put
through its paces by some mysterious but intrepid
inventor.[10]

Although the clandestine nature of this statement seems
both incredible and intriguing, how much more incredible
would it be than the literal idea that the craft in question
were extraterrestrial, assuming of course that reports
of its presence were more than mere newspaper hoaxes?
Again, however, we must remember that Danelek and
others have pointed out already how a number of respectable local officials and other individuals had claimed to
see the "craft" during the Sacramento event, whatever
it actually was. Additionally, despite the view that journalists of the 19th century were held to less scrupulosity
than those in media today, the newspapers reporting the
story at the time *did* have similar reputations to uphold;
it seems the story of an airship drifting through the night
skies above Sacramento would hardly have been considered worthy of the front page, had it been the result of

mere tomfoolery. And yet, in a few instances, this story *had* actually been a front-page feature. Obviously, somebody felt there was real merit to the entire story.

Finally, it would serve us well to note here the exploits of David Schwarz, the Croatian inventor who managed to design an airship that, though not entirely functional, was at least similar in design to reports of the object seen over parts of the United States between 1896 and 1897. On November 3, 1897, one of the designs procured by Schwarz (who, sadly, had died shortly before attempts at taking his design to the air were successful) did manage to become airborne with a degree of success during a test flight at Tempelhof near Berlin, Germany.[11] While Schwarz's work could hardly have matched the ingenuity displayed by the airship being seen around the same time over America, it does show us that others were experimenting with this sort of technology by the late 1890s and were even achieving limited success with their designs. And yet, as Danelek notes in his subsequent book, *Phantoms of the Skies: The Lost History of Aviation from Antiquity to the Wright Brothers,* his interactions with many aviation historians showed that a general knowledge of the experiments of Schwarz and others around the late 19th century remains curiously absent.[12] In other words, these more obscure escapades in the history of human flight, although very real and historically accurate, are just clandestine enough to remain unknown by many otherwise-well-researched experts in the field of avionics and machine-driven aircraft today.

Though such exploration of our hidden history of air travel may be interesting, some would ask what even the most thorough understanding of clandestine aviation history might lend to the understanding of modern UFOs. Furthermore, how could this concept contribute at all to ideas like a coming technological Singularity, or the future of air travel and space flight?

What must be taken into consideration here is that, whereas we are constantly applying Occam's Razor and looking to space and the outer cosmos for answers to the strange things we occasionally see in the skies, we less often look at the obvious clues right here in our midst. In truth, even many of the finest historians and researchers are simply limited in terms of knowing where and what to look for, due to the specialized nature of their studies in any particular given field. Hence, it's often the case that writers, researchers, and journalists, though lacking in the scientific expertise of a well-trained specialist in one subject or another, will have the tendency to look beyond the confines of their niche in their quest for facts and details. Hence, they also may become exposed to a far broader range of subjects, and thus those little details in their minutiae do begin to emerge in ways that others simply may not see.

When it comes to UFOs, we have generally become so entrenched with the idea that we are dealing with the obvious presence of interplanetary visitors from a distant star system that we seldom stop to consider whether seemingly exotic technologies could have their origins here on Earth. By the middle part of the last century, people had begun to look back to the seemingly fantastic airship reports of the 1890s, and had begun to suppose (according to popular UFO-related lines of thought from the 1940s onward) that these reports may have been early encounters with extraterrestrial aircraft. This explanation is far easier to digest than the idea that someone here in our midst could have been doing unique things with existing technology around 1896, and thus might have achieved things that, according to many at the time, would have been considered utterly impossible. But once we incorporate knowledge of what aviation principles were indeed being utilized already close to the end of the 1800s, we can certainly begin to suppose that a scenario involving private industry, perhaps funded by wealthy investors from the West Coast, as Danelek supposes, would seem even more likely than alien visitors.

In other words, part of our ultimate understanding of the UFO mystery may rely less on leaping to conclusions about alien visitors, or even secret government projects. In truth, there may have been a number of secret *private enterprises* throughout the years, which might have contributed to reports of unexplainable and otherworldly looking things in the skies. Similarly, could we suppose that such trends might have continued throughout the decades, and that advanced technologies might also be in production behind the scenes today?

Indeed, thinking along these lines may compliment the incorporation of advanced future science into the equation, just as well. Consider the oft-espoused axiom, invoked recently by a television producer I had been chatting with over the phone, which supposes how government technology is always at least two decades ahead of what the public knows about. If this were indeed true—and history has shown, to some extent, that it is—then we may also need to consider more carefully the ideas of the proponents of a coming Singularity in this context. Ray Kurzweil, among others, speculates that the beginnings of technologies that will eventually lead to smarter-than-human artificial intelligence will begin to emerge within *the next two decades*.[13] Furthermore, a host of other unforeseeable technological innovations will likely begin to contribute to exotic infrastructure that, by many accounts, would seem very much like the sorts of things already described in UFO literature. If Kurzweil is right, does this mean that someplace here on Earth, and at this very moment, various kinds of "secret" technology may already be nearing a technological merging between man and machine? Perhaps even stranger than the idea of a Singularity occurring behind the scenes today is the notion that exotic technologies may have already been in development for some time now. For all we know, the humble emergence of those clumsy "mystery airships" more than a century ago could represent the chronological beginnings of a series of innovations that would eventually far exceed the capabilities of those known to even the most well-educated aviation historians among us today. Depending on the level of technological sophistication such "secret groups" might have achieved, these could also have contributed to a host of reports of strange unidentified flying objects seen as far back as prior to World War I. As Danelek puts it, "The history of manned flight may be far richer and more remarkable—and incomplete—than we can begin to appreciate."[14]

Then again, even if interplanetary beings *are* actually the denizens that haunt those strange flying saucers we keep hearing about, understanding the progression of technology as it applies to technological Singularity still may aid us in understanding what kinds of exotic technologies, even of the *alien* variety, we may actually be dealing with. For all we know, what I've outlined here, in terms of how Singularity might begin to occur on Earth, could have already taken place in some capacity elsewhere in the cosmos; thus, any "aliens" visiting Earth would almost inevitably also represent some kind of post-Singularity intelligence—though for now, we'll save the discussion of alien Singularitarians for later.

On the morning of July 5, 1947, a rancher named Mac Brazel and his son headed out together to collect strange "clusters" of some unknown debris that had appeared around a New Mexico homestead where Brazel was foreman, located 30 miles north of a town called Roswell. The place would forever be remembered for its connection with the alleged government cover-up that ensued, which was said to have involved a crashed flying saucer. This, despite remaining in obscurity until the rekindled interest it received from nuclear physicist Stanton Friedman in 1978, would secure its place as one of the most enigmatic UFO cases in American history.

That same morning back in 1947, the following news brief first appeared in the *Los Angeles Examiner,* describing the recollections of a reputable, if not somewhat unlikely source, who claimed he had witnessed the demonstration of some variety of highly advanced "saucer" technology two decades earlier:

INVENTOR'S TEST OF "FLYING SAUCERS" HERE IN 1928 BARED:
Leo Bentz, one time builder of automobiles, said that he and a friend saw a confidential demonstration of a saucer-like flying model in Griffith Park in 1928. The inventor was George de Bay, interested in a new principle for airplanes. De Bay produced drawings showing designs of contrivance that would skip through the air like a flat stone—an upside down saucer that worked on a vacuum principle requiring ten times less power for propulsion. Inventor de Bay, it is believed, may have gone to Russia.[15]

Whether or not the auto designer ever really witnessed this bizarre demonstration, let alone what may have become of this alleged George de Bay character, remains a mystery. Of course, the notion that he had likely expatriated was a natural conclusion for the time; immediately following World War II, the sudden surge in reports of "flying saucers" had greatly increased paranoia that the world's emerging superpowers, namely the United States and Russia, might have begun to harness highly advanced new propulsion systems for exotic-looking flying vehicles. Although the suspicions about enemy technologies would later seemingly be supplanted (albeit a bit strangely) by the scientific consensus that Earth was under visitation by extraterrestrials, it is clear that earlier explanations for UFOs and their identity had dealt with earthly causes. With his unconventional research into the history of Nazism, historian and researcher Joseph P. Farrell has brought to light a number of reports from immediately after the war, in which claims had been made that saucer-shaped aircraft were being produced toward the end of the conflict. One source for claims along these lines appeared on March 27, 1950, in the Italian newspaper *Il Mattino dell' Italia Centrale*. The article featured a curious account where Guiseppe Belluzzo, an Italian turbine expert and ex-fascist member of Mussolini's government, claimed that designs for Nazi "flying saucers" had been in the works by 1942, first entering production in Italy, and then in Germany. Though the craft in production had never reached a state of functionality before the end of the war, Belluzzo claimed that "by 1950 it had been sufficiently developed to deliver an atom bomb."[16]

Farrell also makes reference to a CIA report, well known in many UFO circles, dated May 27, 1954. In it, even more extraordinary claims of advanced "saucer" technology had been revealed:

A German newspaper recently published an interview with George Klein, famous German engineer and aircraft expert, describing the experimental construction of "flying saucers" carried out by him from 1941 to 1945. Klein stated that he was present when, in 1945, the first piloted "flying saucer" took off and reached a speed of 13,000 miles per hour within three minutes. The experiments resulted in three designs: one designed by (Dr. Richard Meithe) was a disc-shaped aircraft, 135 feet in diameter, which did not rotate; another designed by Habermohl and Schriever, consisted of a large rotating ring, in the centre of which was a round, stationary cabin for the crew. When the Soviets occupied Prague, the Germans destroyed every trace of the "flying saucer" project and nothing more was heard of Habermohl and his assistants.[17]

We must keep in mind that Farrell himself has stressed that all such claims from the immediate post-war era were likely aimed at "cashing in" on the apparent presence of UFOs for purposes of psychological warfare and propaganda, rather than representing *actual* instances where advanced aircraft had been created here on Earth. (This is not to say, however, that such aircraft weren't developed later on, and in other locales.) Nonetheless, it is interesting to note also that Farrell occasionally makes use of the term *technological explosion*, which bears similarity to the concept of a Singularity-style intelligence explosion, when referencing technological innovations that had been taking place during World War II in Nazi Germany. Among these, we find projects that included, among other things, production of functional, combat-tested night vision technology, Kevlar material, miniaturization of broadcast television equipment, and even the possibility that the Nazis may have undertaken uranium enrichment toward the end of the conflict.[18] These will be of certain interest to those of us focused on the potential for rapidly occurring technological innovation within a short period. Let us remember that it is, at the very least, one part of the equation that would begin to constitute a Singularity-style "explosion" of technology. And yet, though the information regarding these sorts of Nazi wartime endeavors is readily available, it is far less often discussed in mainstream history books. Somehow, the details continue to be overshadowed by the more blatant and gory elements constituting the greatest international conflict in modern times.

But amidst the scant and somewhat spurious stories involving "Foo Fighters" and other airborne anomalies that occasionally pepper wartime reports, there are other incidents that may prove to be far more troubling and that suggest there indeed must have been *something* very strange going on, perhaps involving some variety of highly advanced technology working behind the scenes. For instance, there are reports not only of strange things seen in the skies like UFOs, but also Soviet reports of strange underwater phenomenon, known today as "quackers," a name that references the sound these objects would occasionally emit, which was similar to a frog's croak. Soviet navy submarines throughout parts of the North Atlantic Ocean reported these odd manifestations after World War II and throughout the height of the Cold War; their identity, however, was never determined conclusively.[19]

There are still more curious phenomenon that occurred during the war years, which point to even stranger, and perhaps more startling potentials. A German language book published in 1993 called *Zeittunnel: Reisen an den Rand der Ewigkeit* (*Time Tunnel: Travel to the Edge of Eternity*) by journalist Ernst Meckelburg related a number of strange wartime disappearances, reported by the British Royal Air Force, the German Luftwaffe, and American pilots during World War II. Among these was a curious and enigmatic tale, related by an American pilot who witnessed the sudden, inexplicable disappearance of a nearby B-25 in mid-flight over northern India in late 1944. Meckelburg's book is, of course, somewhat difficult to obtain elsewhere in the world, although the witnesses' story in question also appeared in *Fate Magazine* several years later, as related by the pilot himself. Still, today the odd affair remains relatively unknown, and even online searches regarding key details pertaining to the strange incident return few, if any, results.

However, on the Wednesday, August 3, 2011, edition of the popular late-night radio program *Coast to*

Coast AM, host George Noory welcomed investigative journalist Leslie Kean to the program to discuss firsthand accounts of UFO reports, which she collected from top military generals and pilots and featured in her book, *UFOs: Generals, Pilots and Government Officials Go On the Record.*[20] During the second hour of Kean's interview on the program, Noory and his guest received a phone call from a 93-year-old World War II veteran and pilot now living in Coos Bay, Oregon, named Stewart. As the caller began to relate his story, it became evident that this was none other than the same pilot who had witnessed the strange, vanishing B-25 incident so many years before in 1944, and his recollection of those events today are still nothing short of haunting.

According to Stewart, during World War II there were many pilots who reported seeing what have traditionally been referred to as Foo Fighters. "My story involves a disappearing B-25," Stewart said[21], reminding his audience that this was the same model of airplane that aviation pioneer Jimmy Doolittle flew over Tokyo in the early part of World War II. "But I'm 93 years old, so have a little patience with me!" he joked.

Stewart explained that he had flown B-25s in the China Burma India Theater of operations during World War II. The disappearance in question took place late in 1944, while he and his wingmen were flying over Northern India toward targets located in Burma against the Japanese. "We were a flight of three B-25s, and I was in the right seat of the lead aircraft," he recalled. As the trio passed over a range of mountains along their route down into Burma, Stewart noted that they encountered "scattered, fluffy little cumulus clouds" at their then-present flight altitude. "As we entered them, the procedure was that the right wingman would rise up 200 feet, and the left wingman would descend 200 feet, so as not to collide in the clouds. I remember the guy on the right—I had flown with him before, his name was Reynard—continued this way, where he would rise up 200 feet, and come back down again. This happened about three or four times, and then he entered a cloud, and did not come out!"

Without warning, nor any other indication that Reynard had experienced trouble, the pilot and his B-25 had apparently just *vanished*. "He was just gone," Stewart said, "so we, the remaining two pilots, contacted each other, and we began turning to the right, circling around hoping to catch sight of him because, certainly, we couldn't conceive of anybody disappearing like that." Despite their attempts at searching for Reynard or his plane, they were unable to locate the missing aircraft.

"Finally, we decided that he might have made a sudden turn to the right and gone back to base, because he might have lost his radio, or something like that. So we continued on, and bombed our targets, and came back to the base." Upon their return, Stewart and the remaining wingman inquired about whether Reynard had returned early, but no one there had seen or heard from the missing pilot either. "He was gone, and so we referred to him as missing, and reported the location to the people at the base. And they sent search planes out, including two R-4 helicopters. We searched for several days afterward. We searched the ground below, hoping to find signs of a crashed airplane. He was reported missing in action, and that's the last we heard of it!

"Later on, I wrote a description of this incident," Stewart said, and, after having it rejected from several publications, *Fate Magazine* finally decided to carry the story. "Maybe a couple of years after that, I got a letter from a man in Germany (Ernst Meckelburg) who was writing a book about disappearing aircraft, because he had many reports from the *Luftwaffe* from that era, and also British aircraft. He had kinda collected their stories, and they were similar to mine, where airplanes just disappear into thin air. He wrote a book called *Zeittunnel*, and sent me a copy of the book, which included my story. His theory, according to *Zeittunnel*, was that there are sorts of parallel universes—that things can go in and out of universes," Stewart explained, "which would account for UFOs, of course."

So far as understanding the greater UFO mystery, there may be several things we can learn from a careful consideration of the reports of unexplained aerial phenomenon that began rising to prominence during and shortly after the World War II years. One aspect of the mystery worthy of mention here is that while the Nazis were honing in on some incredibly advanced scientific and technological principles during the War, it is obvious that the Allied Forces were doing the same; how else, we can argue, would they have prevailed over the conflict?

With this in mind, is it possible that, although certain varieties of exotic UFO activity may have been taking place much earlier than World War II, it was during this pivotal period, as a result of the demand for wartime innovation, which many of the necessary technologies began to appear that, quite literally, *allowed* perception of certain UFO phenomenon? For instance, though Hanz Geiger developed the first full functional Geiger counters for detection of radiation as far back as 1908, it wasn't until 1947 that Sidney Liebson, who had participated in Pacific bomb tests, managed to create a lower-voltage halogen counter that operated more effectively in the detection of ionizing radiation.[22] That same year, Liebson received his PhD from the University of Maryland, and, of course, 1947 would also usher in the modern UFO era with reports of "flying saucers," the likes of those seen by Kenneth Arnold in June of that year.

Liebson would go on to receive an award from the U.S. Navy that involved another wartime technology that allowed improved ability to perceive exotic technologies in our midst. This, of course, involved the use of radar systems. Prior to the war, the major countries in both the Allied Nations and the Axis Powers had worked toward perfecting radar technologies similar to those in use today, with countries such as Canada and Australia developing their own during the conflict.[23] Though we can say that certain varieties of radar *did* exist prior to the Second World War, it cannot be refuted that the technology would not be perfected until this very demanding period in our modern history.

Indeed, we see that an argument has begun to appear where, in the event that at least some UFOs did represent technologies that were not created on Earth during or immediately after the war years, humankind may simply have lacked the sophisticated applications necessary to observe them effectively prior to World War II. Maintaining this same line of thought, we might just as well say that the emergence of another kind of devastating technology during this period—atomic weaponry—might have caused our once-dim and uninteresting planet to have shone like a brilliant beacon through space, thus calling attention to a new race in the universe capable of harnessing the power of the atom. Based on this, we might also consider that any advanced technological society similar to us, had they become aware that a more primitive culture elsewhere in the universe had begun experimenting with atomic weaponry, might take interest in such dangerous new Earthly affairs.

But there are problems with leaping to the conclusion that the technology in question must have been extraterrestrial in nature. Rather obviously, when UFO reports began to be called into question seriously by scientists in the late

1940s and early 1950s, humankind had not yet managed to escape Earth's own atmosphere. In other words, having not yet succeeded in reaching outer space, Occam's Razor would again favor the notion that, because these exotic vessels are seen flying through the skies, they must come from outer space. Whenever possible, as philosopher Bertrand Russell and others have paraphrased, we seem to build constructions within our minds from known entities, which are then substituted in place of those things that remain unknown. Quite simply, we knew what UFOs were capable of, but we didn't know *where* they were from, so we began leaping to conclusions that have permeated and stereotyped the serious study of unidentified objects in our skies ever since.

Considering all the available potentials, whether UFOs were from here on Earth or from outer space, it is clear that they began to rise to prevalence as a cultural phenomenon during and immediately after World War II. Thus, the work of novelist Mack Maloney managed to garner my attention, following the publication of an interesting non-fiction offering in 2011 called *UFOs in Wartime*. Mack's general premise with this book was that UFO sightings and activity seem to increase during military conflicts. But exactly why is this the case? If it were for military purposes, thinking back to the reports of Foo Fighters and strange objects witnessed during World War II, and these strange craft were of terrestrial origin, why would they not have intervened in various aerial battles? Indeed, a majority, if not virtually all reports of World War II Foo Fighters place these strange objects well enough out of reach, as if they had merely been interested in *observing* our military activities. Does this lead us back to the premise that UFO craft must have been alien in origin?

Perhaps not. Again, with regard to exotic (or seemingly exotic) technology coming to fruition during the Second World War, the premise that these might have been some kind of highly advanced Nazi technology has always seemed to remain a plausible, though also somewhat elusive possibility. During a conversation I had with Maloney in early 2012, I asked him exactly what his feelings were regarding a possible source behind reports of UFOs with regard to a link to Nazis and advanced propulsion methods they may have been developing for aircraft. In Maloney's opinion, this was unlikely for five primary reasons[24]:

1. There are no instances where Foo Fighters were reported firing on American or British bombers or other aircraft.

2. Much the same, there are no reports of these unidentified craft firing on grounded soldiers or ships at sea.

3. By 1943, dwindling resources in Nazi Germany would have made it unlikely that they could have obtained the kinds of supplies needed to construct advanced aircraft along the lines of purported Foo Fighters.

4. Had the Nazis been producing advanced saucer-shaped or other kinds of advanced aircraft with anti-gravitational capabilities, the Allies would have discovered an operation following the war on par with America's Manhattan Project. Little, if any evidence for an operation of this magnitude was ever found.

5. At the end of the war, German scientists were distributed between Russia and the United States. Those that came to America, such as Werner Von Braun, worked closely with NASA and the American space program. It would seem highly unlikely that German rocket scientists, had they been aware of advanced propulsion methods during the War, would not supply this information for the eventual efforts toward entering outer space.

"My final point," Maloney said, "is that, if the Germans had this kind of incredible super weapon technology, then why did they lose the war?" Indeed, if technology existed that could have presented the Nazis with such an advanced ability to outmaneuver enemy aircraft, it does not seem likely that this technology would be used so ineffectively in combat. On the other hand, we cannot discount the stories of Foo Fighters altogether; the truth seems to be lost to us someplace between two primary facts: that while Foo Fighters may have existed, they did not appear to be of known human origin.

Let us consider the previous statement entailing objects of *known human origin,* once more, and this time perhaps more carefully. Indeed, we are reasonably certain that humans during the 1940s were not involved in the production of aircraft that could account for the Foo Fighter reports. Alternatively, we have explored earlier in this chapter the possibility that *secret* advanced technologies might occasionally undergo development as a result of private industrial interests. However, the idea that any private agency could have garnered the resources needed for this in the midst of a global conflict—in addition to somehow managing to carry on a secret, highly advanced (and thus, very costly) project such as this *behind the scenes*—seems almost ludicrous. Thus, it begins to become clear why scientists in the post-war years were so eager to commit to belief in an extraterrestrial source. After all, these things couldn't be our own, could they?

"So if not Nazi technology," I asked Mack during our discussion, "what were they?"

"I don't know. I think that when I first started doing the book *UFOs in Wartime,* I really didn't know, and I guess that I was just thinking along the lines of extraterrestrials, like everyone else. Since doing the book, doing the research, and just talking about it now for the last three or four months, I'm really coming around to a different idea."

"What else could they be?" I asked. "What's your theory?"

"My theory now is that these things represent time travelers from our own future, who are coming back to see history as it's being made."

Maloney admitted that he was hardly the first to come to this sort of conclusion. However, this idea nonetheless seemed most likely, to him, due to a number of criteria it could potentially explain:

> You obviously have a technology, somewhere, that created these Foo Fighters, that demonstrated these unbelievable characteristics like flying incredibly fast, appearing and disappearing, and so forth. If *you* had that kind of technology, then why would you choose to ride 100 feet off the wing of a Lancaster bomber as it's bombing Berlin in the middle of the night, with anti-aircraft fire going on all around you, night fighters, and all the confusion and utter chaos of combat? Why would you do that, unless you wanted to be there to see history as it's being made? That theory fits in a lot of holes with regard to what UFOs are, and frankly, I think it fills in more holes in the puzzle than the "little green men from Mars" theory. That's what I'm leaning towards, is that they *are* time travelers from our own future, coming back to see history as it's being made.

Admittedly, this idea is where a lot of people tend to get lost when it comes down to offering *plausible* theories as to what kinds of technology could be behind the UFO enigma. Modern physics remains in a skeptically fueled game of tug-o-war over the issue of whether literal travel through time could even be possible (as we began to outline already in the previous chapter). But the theory has nonetheless proven to be an attractive one among many in the field. Recall again Whitley Strieber's notion from earlier that the figures from his own abduction experiences might have been time travelers—and humans, no less— assuming the disguise of extraterrestrial visitors.

For all we know, a humanity several decades—or perhaps even several *centuries*—from now might appear quite alien to us. In fact, if the kinds of changes anticipated by the futurists of today do indeed occur, there may also be little need for any kind of "disguises," either. We, as the humans of today, are painfully bound to the limits of our perception as biological entities. The "humans" of tomorrow, having mastered the integration of machinery and advanced synthetic sciences into the very fabric of our species, may not only *look* very different, but could also be freed from the bounds of natural limitation that our biology imposes. These humans may have mastered technologies that, though existent, remain in their infancy today, ranging from genetic hybridization between different animal species, to functional telepathy and other psychic abilities. These future humans—or *homo mechanicus*, to borrow the name bestowed on them by my colleague Dr. Maxim Kammerer—might be an entirely new species, of sorts—the direct result of an intelligent race that had taken evolution into its own hands. Beings such as these may indeed be capable of seeing past the illusions that space and time place before humans today, and their visions, as well as perhaps their abilities to *manipulate* their reality, could present circumstances that you or I would have great difficulty understanding, whether that may involve direct manipulation of the flow of time, or other wild and frightening prospects.

Albeit somewhat within the framework of an extra-terrestrial model, the astute Dr. J. Allen Hynek seemed to describe almost *perfectly* such an advanced civilization decades ago:

> I hold it entirely possible that a technology exists, which encompasses both the physical and the psychic, the material and the mental. There are stars that are millions of years older than the sun. There may be a civilization that is millions of years more advanced than man's. We have gone from Kitty Hawk to the moon in some seventy years, but it's possible that a million-year-old civilization may know something that we don't.... I hypothesize an "M&M" technology encompassing the mental and material realms. The psychic realms, so mysterious to us today, may be an ordinary part of an advanced technology.[25]

Although that advanced technology may not exist here among us today (at least in an accessible way), it could very well be that parts of what we perceive now as some variety of alien technology are, in fact, something of our very own.

They are the playthings, in a sense, of our eventual progeny.

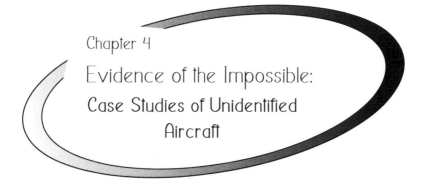

Chapter 4

Evidence of the Impossible:
Case Studies of Unidentified
Aircraft

*I'll give you the facts—all of the facts—
you decide.*

—Edward J. Ruppelt,
The Report on Unidentified Flying Objects

The year 1973 was pivotal in history for many, especially in the United States. The floodgates that had been holding back the Watergate scandal surrounding Richard Nixon and his staff began to break open, and by late March the last remaining U.S. soldiers involved in the prolonged and murky Vietnam conflict had finally returned home. The World Trade Center, which in the post-9/11 world of today will remain an icon of American perseverance in times of trouble, was first opened to the public in April of that year. Summer would follow, bringing with it one of the longest full solar eclipses of the entire millennium, bathing the Earth in darkness for more than seven minutes. And only a few months later, in November, NASA would launch the 84-day *Skylab 4* mission, consisting of three astronauts propelled toward the orbiting Space Station on a Saturn IB rocket.

November 1973 would also prove to be a pivotal time in the lives of a handful of youthful commuters, who had been traveling along a lonely stretch of highway late one evening among the rolling hills of Georgia's Piedmont Plateau. Though incredibly, although the circumstances here *did* involve some variety of advanced aircraft, one thing is certain: No Saturn rocket, or any other kind of well-known manmade vehicle, can account for what was seen.

It was just after midnight on a Sunday in late November, and 20-year-old Mike Reese was driving north along Highway 23/42 toward his home in Forest Park, just south of Atlanta, Georgia. Mike's wife, his sister, Pam, his newborn daughter, and Pam's two young girls were all with him in the car—a 1963 aquamarine Dodge Polara with a push-button transmission—returning together from a weekend visit with his wife's parents in nearby Monticello. Having just passed the town of Jackson, a light fog had begun to drift through the valley, and the chilly night air had kept them awake as they peered across the landscape, growing ever nearer to their next junction, a little town called Locust Grove. From here, they had planned to take the short Bill Gardner Parkway over to Interstate 75—a regular route for them—and one they would follow the rest of the way home. Though they were making good time, work would arrive very early tomorrow for Mike, who at the time had a job with the Georgia Division of Transportation.

It was just 5 or so miles outside of Locust Grove that Mike first noticed the bright light hovering in the distance. Glancing to his right, the object had caught his attention as it began moving over a mountain ridge to the east, drifting silently over the hills and valleys between.

Mike had wondered aloud to the others what a helicopter might be doing flying so late in the evening. The typical considerations all leapt to mind: Maybe someone had gotten lost while hiking, or maybe the helicopter was looking for some suspicious vehicle reported in the area. Perhaps they were airlifting the victim of some accident to a nearby hospital; or maybe it was some kind of military helicopter passing through on a late-night routine. As Mike and his company traveled along, it became apparent by the direction the light was moving that it would eventually cross with their path of travel. The object drew closer, and Mike was eventually able to see that the orientation of lights it displayed was not like any standard pattern he had ever witnessed on conventional aircraft. Within minutes, they were passing through Locust Grove, but as their exit onto the Bill Gardner Parkway approached on their left, Mike opted to continue north along Highway 23/42, just to get a better look at whatever this mysterious flying object might turn out to be.

The group continued traveling in the direction of the light, with Mike watching carefully for a location where he might pull over and observe the strange craft. Although there were a few trees lining the sides of the road, the light the craft had been giving off made its location obvious. Ahead on the left, Mike could see a power sub-station, surrounded on all sides by chain link fencing, and as he and the others drew near, it became clear that the object was hovering directly over this facility. Mike hurried along, and once they reached the clearing where the station was built, they suddenly found themselves in full view of this incredible aircraft.

It was enormous—a massive, disk-shaped object with colored lights along its perimeter, hovering in perfect silence above the power station, and probably in full view of any commuters on the nearby Interstate.

Mike sped into the driveway in front of the gate at the station, rapidly flashing his headlights off and on before leaping out of the car into the cold November night. In the sky above him, he could see the craft in all its vivid detail, suspended virtually motionless directly above. It was, by all accounts, a flying saucer, with its colored lights rotating along its outer edges. Though he could not discern the color of the craft itself with certainty, Mike guessed that it was probably dull silver. Judging from the width of the fencing around the station, Mike estimated that the craft was at least 100 to 150 feet in diameter, and hovering between 200 to 250 feet above them.

Mike's wife and sister couldn't believe what was happening. Not only was there a huge, alien-looking saucer looming right over them, but they had watched helplessly as Mike pulled off to the side of the road, apparently signaling to the craft with his flashing headlights, then jumping out as he began waving his arms at this thing. What had he been thinking? Both women became very upset at seeing this, and their terrified shouting could be heard as they urged Mike to get back in the car and get them all out of there.

Mike, on the other hand, was intent on trying to get the attention of whoever may have been on board that saucer. "I continued waving my arms, as if to say to them, *Hey, I want to see who is flying this machine,*" Mike recounted to me later. "The craft was just in a suspended state with these lights going around it. I remember thinking to myself, *I have to remember this,* so I likened the lights to the sort you would see on a Christmas tree, being red, green, and blue."[1]

Though the colors could be discerned, something about those lights still managed to escape any kind of easy description. Mike strained his eyes to see what the actual source of each illumination may have been, comparing them to portholes along the side of a sailing vessel. He guessed each "porthole" was probably 18–24 inches in diameter, and spaced 8 to 12 feet apart. The lights would emit from these portholes in sequence with a first color, then a second as the first light slowly faded, illuminating the next nearest porthole in the new color, and then on to a third before repeating in this way all along the perimeter of the craft. "The lights seemed to me as if there was a white light inside that rotated, and would strike the portholes that were encased with the different colored transparent materials," Mike's e-mail said. "The best way I can describe these portholes is like the embers in a camp fire; a glowing type of light. That's how my mind put it into perspective."[2]

The craft lingered there, completely silent and motionless, for another one or two minutes before it slowly began to drift toward the west, eventually passing right over I-75. Once the object was no longer in view, Mike returned to his car, finding his wife and sister still very terrified by what was happening. Mike took several minutes trying to calm them down. Finally, after the excitement died down somewhat, the six of them resumed their journey home, driving the rest of the way in almost complete silence.

"We were all in some sort of shock," Mike wrote of the incident. "When I got back to the house, I called Atlanta's Action 5 New Channel," which, according to his sister, had featured stories about similar sightings in the area around that time. "They hung up on me."[3]

Mike first contacted me in June 2011, nearly four decades after the incident. After a number of correspondences where we discussed the particulars of the UFO he had seen (as well as a few other peculiar experiences from throughout his life), I decided to make arrangements to meet him, primarily so we could further discuss a few of the details surrounding the 1973 Locust Grove encounter. In the years following the incident, Mike indicated that he had often found it difficult to describe this experience to people. "They can't digest this type of information," he told me, recalling how he had shared the entire series of events with a coworker shortly after the encounter.[4] Like Mike, this individual had held an interest in astronomy growing up, and the two of them often talked about things they had observed in the night sky through telescopes throughout the years. On this occasion however, as Mike told what he and his family had seen over the power substation in Locust Grove, he watched as the expression on his friend's face drooped with disbelief. The rest of the day, Mike became the recipient of frequent uneasy glances from this individual. It didn't take many more exchanges like this for Mike to feel that he might do well to simply forget anything had ever happened at all—or at least act as though he had.

Today, people's perception of subjects like UFOs has changed a great deal, especially compared with the early 1970s. In those days, what we have come to know as the modern UFO era was barely two decades old, and reports of encounters with physical occupants of such craft were still only in their infancy. In fact, one of the more striking early incidents that involved physical beings from an alleged UFO had taken place just weeks before Mike's encounter, six hours south of Locust Grove in the Gulf Coast town of Pascagoula, Mississippi. It was there on October 11th that two coworkers named Charles Hickson and Calvin Parker had been night fishing for speckled trout and redfish by an area known as the old Shaupeter Shipyard. The men observed a blue light in the sky, which came down very near to them, hovering over the bayou, revealing a large football-shaped object. Then an opening appeared in the craft, from which three alien-looking beings emerged, floating above the ground over to where Parker and Hickson were fishing. The men were terrified of what was happening, but were not able to resist capture and were taken onto the craft. While on board, the two were examined by a device resembling a large human eye, and were eventually returned to the dock where they had been fishing. Both men had been so frightened by what happened that Hickson initially warned Parker that they should never tell anyone what happened. After a few hours, the two eventually relented and took their story to Pascagoula Sheriff Fred Diamond.[5] Interestingly, during the period between Mike Reese's first mention of his 1973 encounter to me in an e-mail and our eventual meeting over dinner in late September 2011, Charles Hickson passed away, at the age of 80. Throughout his life, he had always maintained that the curious and terrifying events from that evening in October 1973 were true and accurate.

Much like Hickson and Parker's reaction to their unusual encounter, for some time Mike Reese had felt it was useless to tell others what he and his family had experienced. In some ways, he also seemed to feel like what he had experienced was clandestine for legitimate reasons. In an e-mail exchange with me on June 9, 2011, Mike shared the following:

> If the government did retrieve things from Roswell and it was alien, I can kind of understand why they would not release this information. Just in the last few days as I think about how to describe this to you, I get into [an] "out of sorts" feeling because my mind is trying to rationalize the incident. I'm not saying that this should not happen; I am saying that a lot of people would be walking around in a daze for a long, long time [if they tried the same thing]. I myself have a strong will and strong mind...but if I pondered over this incident long, I would probably lose everything.[6]

This sentiment Mike expressed, involving the trouble associated with pondering the more curious elements of the UFO enigma, is very prevalent in the study of unexplained phenomenon, particularly with UFOs. Those who are "gifted" with an otherworldly experience seldom see it as such, and can easily become inundated with fear of the unknown, much like Hickson and Parker had been. In fact, only hours after their abduction experience, the two were left in a room where they were secretly recorded, following their discussion with Sheriff Fred Diamond. Rather than making any mention of a hoax or prank, Parker—obviously still very shaken—repeatedly told Hickson he wanted to see a doctor. Even after Hickson had left the room, Parker could be heard saying aloud to himself that, "It's hard to believe.... Oh God, it's awful.... I know there's a God up there."[7]

In closing, Mike assured me that "this stuff is very real," and that it "did happen as I described it."[8] Additionally, he accepted my offer to meet in person, and to bring his sister along, who had also agreed to speak with me. "I'm sure she would not mind giving you her description of the incident."[9]

After a few weeks of planning between our schedules, I finally arranged to meet Mike and his sister, Pam, along with a few other family members and associates for dinner on September 24, 2011. It was a beautiful, colorful drive through early autumn at around sunset that evening, and the Nantahala National Forest's high ridges and deep gorges carried me along to the town of Murphy,

North Carolina, where Mike now lives. Two associates of mine, Chris Heyes and Matthew Oakley, came along, too, because they are co-hosts on my weekly Web radio program, *The Gralien Report*. I felt they might be helpful in gathering information while we shared dinner and a few glasses of wine with Mike and his company. Though we arrived late, Mike and the others greeted us warmly, having reserved a table for us in a private room in the back of the restaurant. Once orders for drinks and entrées had been made, our conversation ensued. (My travel companions ordered martinis, and I ordered a glass of one of the café's fine pinot noirs.)

As I had anticipated, there were a number of what I took to be interesting secondary details about the incident that came to light while discussing the encounter in person. Mike's description of the events remained remarkably consistent, and his sister Pam, who sat beside me the entire evening, agreed with Mike on nearly every point. Pam was quieter than Mike, however, and though she was willing to share details about her own experiences, there was still an underlying tension or hesitation I sensed from her, especially while discussing the Locust Grove incident. Mike also mentioned that he had experienced intermittent headaches and nausea in the days following the encounter. "After the incident in Locust Grove, I had an extreme headache sometime after. I even had to stop on the side of the road while I was going to work at GA-DOT and throw up."[10] Mike was puzzled by the sudden illness, and told me he "had to go to the infirmary to get checked out," where he was told he was experiencing an optical headache. "I can't remember how long after the incident this headache occurred."[11] He told me that his recollection of this aspect of the encounter came after reading an article I had written online, where I described headaches following other people's UFO sightings. Indeed, this subject was familiar to me. Mike's own circumstances, especially the headaches and nausea, sounded similar to some of the various symptoms of radiation sickness, which can follow exposure to small doses of ionizing radiation.

Another interesting aspect of Mike's circumstance involved his recollection of reading a story only a few years before the Locust Grove incident that was remarkably similar to his own encounter: "I remember reading in one of the *Fate Magazine* issues years ago of a sighting that also involved the craft hovering over a power sub-station."[12] In my personal library, I have a number of volumes of *Fate Magazine* dating as far back as 1959; however, scanning through issues from the 1960s, I was unable to locate the article Mike described. Nonetheless, this aspect of the story is of interest, due in part to the fact that Mike even wondered how this knowledge of similar circumstances— obtained *prior* to seeing the object over Locust Grove— might have influenced what he and the others had seen. This hints at a very strange and complicated area with the UFO enigma, that involves the apparently *interactive* nature of many UFO reports; some witnesses even express feeling that their roles as observers alone could play some part in the appearance of various physical qualities UFOs display.

"When I saw the craft in Locust Grove, I remember thinking to myself that the craft is drawing some type of energy from the station."[13] Mike described the way the craft had positioned itself directly over the power facility, unmoving except for the rotating lights along the rim of the craft. Holding its position in this way, he described this as being what he called a sort of static mode. "Maybe this craft has the ability to draw energy from external sources, and the colored lights are a product of this," he guessed.[14]

Mike further speculated that the color configuration of the lights rotating around the craft could have resulted in the craft appearing as a single, white light from a distance. Guessing that the saucer's outer rim acted as a centrifuge, perhaps spinning more quickly as it accelerated, Mike suggested that when the craft's rotation changed from the "static" state into a "hyper mode" that visually white light may result. "This would probably make some sort of sense, since most sightings that are seen at night are white light,"[15] he said, recalling also that the object he witnessed had first appeared as either a white or bright orange light as it initially became visible to he and his family over the mountains in the distance. Based on the function of the craft he witnessed, this notion complements a general *additive color model* for light, where red, green, and blue light can be combined to produce other colors. If one of these primary colors is blended with another in equal amounts, it is possible to create secondary additive colors that include yellow, cyan, or magenta. Combining all three primary colors of visible light in equal measure will produce white light.[16] Could it be mere coincidence that the colors Mike and the others saw on the craft happened to be the additive primary colors of the visible light spectrum?

This understanding of visible light and its behavior was first credited to Scottish mathematical physicist James Clerk Maxwell, whose research provided many of the fundamentals for modern theories of how electric and magnetic fields interact with matter.[17] Ironically, Maxwell's own interest in colored light prompted him to design, of all things, a *rotating disk*, as well as a "color box" that he used to help discern the inner workings of additive color mixing. Maxwell's inspiration for the use of a disk-shaped device in this way may have stemmed, at least in part, from an earlier experiment he described in his ground-laying work, *A Treatise on Electricity and Magnetism*. This involved the French physicist Dominique Arago's discovery that "a magnet placed near a rotating metallic disk experiences a force tending to make it follow the motion of the disk," despite there being no such interaction when the metal surface and the magnet are at rest.[18] Arago first discovered this effect in 1825, formulating a simple device based on his observations where a compass needle was placed on a pivot above a circular piece of copper, which he turned using a hand crank attached to the device. Of particular interest to Arago was the observation that the proximity between the two had an unusual effect of reducing the influence of Earth's magnetic field on the compass needle.

After consulting with a few colleagues who were equipped with far more expertise in the fields of electricity and magnetism than I presently wield, I came to the determination that, although my deductions based on Maxwell and Arago's research could represent possible factors involving the propulsion of the Locust Grove UFO, the multitude of other unknown elements involved here (its specific dimensions, the various materials the craft had been built with, its exact weight, and so forth) could easily modify or make unlikely the basic mechanism I had begun to envision. In other words, given the perceptual limitations of any single, standalone encounter such as this, we are provided with only bits and pieces of information, each pointing to more specific possibilities as to how such a craft might function. Therefore, I should say right up-front that I recognize the potential flaws any set of unknown circumstances might cause in attempts at understanding a craft like this. Still, the Arago effect, which involves long-known, tested, and valid observations, may nonetheless hold a key to understanding some aspects regarding the operation of the strange saucer Mike witnessed. If I had to admit that intuition of any kind was involved in this determination, I could say it's a gut feeling, if nothing else.

Thus, stopping to consider the behavior of the object seen over Locust Grove in 1973, especially compared with Maxwell and Arago's observations of electricity and magnetism in relation to spinning disks, a number of parallels do begin to emerge. If this UFO craft were indeed designed to reduce the natural influence Earth's magnetic field would exert against it, then it is likely that the technology Mike and the others observed may utilize a more thorough understanding than most, with regard to the curious interrelationship between electricity, magnetism, and gravity. Although some speculate that these forces may literally be distinct observable effects of a single, fundamental, and universal energy source, our scientific ability to discern between these, or manipulate them independently, still remains incomplete. True, a highly advanced technology—whether alien, or stemming from some variety of human origin—that has mastered the manipulation of electricity and magnetism would no doubt have solved this great riddle of the sciences; the behavior the Locust Grove craft exhibited indeed might hint at a technology that could also manipulate gravity.[19]

Regarding Mike's own ideas as to how this craft might have operated, I feel it is relevant now to include some of his background information, excerpted from a resume Mike shared with me, detailing both his educational and military background. In 1972, he completed his study of mechanical drafting at the Atlanta Area Technical Institute; this was followed in 1978 by studies in pre- engineering curriculum at Georgia College in

Milledgeville, Georgia. Between 1982 and 1985, Reese went on to study architectural engineering at the Southern Technical Institute, located in Marietta, Georgia. Finally, in 2000, he obtained his present certification as a North Carolina Licensed General Contractor at Southwestern Community College. At the time of our first meeting, he was also undergoing a series of business and entrepreneurship classes at Tri-County Community College.

Regarding his military service, between 1975 and 1978 Reese was a member of the U.S. Army. He served positions at Fort Knox, Kentucky, and Fort Carson, Colorado, in addition to a position in Dexheim, Germany. Reese's expertise was primarily that of a combat engineer and tank crew member. He was honorably discharged following his service, during which he obtained confidential clearance.

With his technical background in both military and civilian sectors, it quickly became evident that Mike Reese has a broad understanding of modern engineering and technical drafting/design. I concluded, with certain confidence, that Mike would have a clear ability to discern and make educated technical observations regarding various kinds of machinery, and with a degree of effectiveness that might exceed that of the average civilian UFO witness. Although the Locust Grove incident predated much of his gathered experience, Mike nonetheless had seemed to carefully recall vivid details of the object he and the others witnessed, and throughout the years that followed, began to apply some of his knowledge in an effort to understand the experience. Thus, after contacting me and discussing his encounter at length, Mike was kind enough to provide me with computer-aided technical drawings of the object, as well as his closest estimates regarding his location in proximity to the craft itself. Additionally, Mike offered to help me in the future by providing similar drawings, based on the observations of other witnesses, particularly when detailed reports or eyewitness sketches were available.

It should also be noted that throughout Mike's life, he was exposed to a number of subjects of interest to researchers of the unexplained, beginning at an early age. Mike was born in 1953 in Murphy, North Carolina. As a child, he was familiar with a variety of esoteric subjects, due mostly to his father's interest in such things as yoga, meditation, spiritualism, and, of course, UFOs. Mike described his father as "an interesting fellow...respected by the peoples in this small town"[20] and an avid reader of magazines like *Fate*. Born in 1893, he was almost twice the age of Mike's mother. "I remember my dad was into Yoga at 60-plus years old, and read a lot of different types of books. He would tell me about how he grew up, and how he witnessed inventions like the airplane, radio, and TV. I began to read a lot of his *Fate* publications, and was very intrigued by the writings, particularly the UFO articles. I would often think, *It would really be awesome to see one of these craft*, but I never thought about how I would react if I did have such an encounter."[21]

Mike also described to me privately a number of experiences from his youth that he felt involved the use of intuition, though he never implied that he believed himself to have intuitive or psychic abilities of his own. Some of these instances involved experiences where he picked up on sensations or strong feelings that later proved to be useful, or even life-saving. Altogether, Mike's orientation regarding his unusual life experiences seemed to be from an entirely logical position. He is a religious man, as are his wife, sister, and other members of the small group that joined us for our late September dinner. But perhaps most incredibly, the Locust Grove incident had not been the only experience Mike had that involved seeing an unidentified flying object. On October 30, 2008, Mike had been traveling late in the day along Highway 515 in the North Georgia Highlands when he witnessed a strange triangular-shaped craft. After his sighting, Mike reported his observations to the Georgia area Mutual UFO Network (MUFON). Following is an excerpt from their database regarding Mike's second encounter:

> An adult male resident of Hayesville N.C. (just above the Georgia state-line in N.C.) was driving along Hwy 515 about 5 miles beyond Blue Ridge. He pulled off to check the load on his truck, and upon getting back in noticed a low oscillating sound he felt might be from the truck, but was apparently not. Looking out through the windshield, the witness observed a triangular object moving to the south perpendicular to Hwy 515 at about 300–400

feet in altitude and moving 40–50mph. The object seemed to be moving with 2 points forward, a dim white light on each forward point, with a white and a red light on the rear point. Witness considered the lights connected (by fuselage) as the background sky was lighter than the craft. The witness did not give an estimate as to distance, but it was close enough to offer the oscillating sound and for him to estimate the lights were about 200–300 feet apart. This witness has agreed to meet with [Field Investigators] Mark and Leslie M. of Blairsville. He is currently working on a sketch and diagram.[22]

Mike told me he likened the Locust Grove UFO to being "the Holy Grail of sightings,"[23] and that the Highway 515 encounter didn't hold nearly as much personal significance as the one in 1973. The MUFON investigators that Mike spoke with told him they believed the object was likely a military craft, because there is a small military base south of the location where Mike had stopped to check the load of his truck.

The night of our dinner meeting, I asked Mike to detail for me both these encounters again while we were together in person. Mike's testimony remained remarkably consistent, especially regarding the Locust Grove incident, which had been the primary focus of our discussion. I only found the details to vary slightly in one area: Pam said her two young girls had been with them the night of the encounter also, asleep in the back seat of the Polara, whereas Mike's initial recollections had involved his newborn daughter being the only child present at the time. Despite her reservation, Pam went on to describe an incident from her teenage years, occurring at around the age of 16, where she had awoken in the middle of the night. As she walked into the living room, through the front windows she had observed several objects she described as blimp or dirigible-shaped near the ground, gliding *above* the highway outside her home. The objects were moving fast and disappeared from view quickly. Though she had recalled this experience in vivid detail, she nonetheless advised me that this might have been some sort of hallucination, because she had just awoken from a deep sleep.

After discussing these and a few other UFO incidents in depth, we spent the remainder of the evening chatting and touching on a variety of subjects, including a family member of Mike's who works in the areas involving intelligence and linguistics. There was a lot of joking and laughter, but regardless of what the subject at any given time may have been, Mike, along with his wife, sister, and the others, were accommodating, enjoyable, and very open with what they shared.

"I'm not worried about this being kept confidential," Mike told me at one point. "I have nothing to hide, and it's the truth. You can use my name if you like," he said with a grin. "I just haven't told too many folks about the Locust Grove encounter, because when I have in the past, they just look at me oddly."[24]

Mike's conclusion regarding what he had seen was resolute. "Either our government or some other organization has some very, *very* sophisticated craft, or there are beings that do come from other places, dimensions, or time."[25] He admitted that he gravitates toward the latter of these possible explanations, and even thanked me for my research involving the subject of UFOs. Little did he know, at that time, how significant his observations had been—especially such notions as a dimensional, or even trans-temporal origin behind some of these UFOs.

"I believe people need to know the truth," he said. "I think you guys are on the edge of revealing more truth to people, if they would listen, than we may expect."[26]

Despite merely being an incredible story, Mike Reese's encounter with a strange, unidentifiable aircraft over Locust Grove, Georgia, in 1973 highlights a number of constants that are present in the field of UFO research today. Any quick search online will turn up countless numbers of similar reports, a good number of which were likely logged by respectable individuals like Mike, who have had remarkable encounters with a technology that they can't explain. Despite this, there are far too many in the scientific community who remain content with dismissing such stories, relishing in their artful mastery of neglect on the grounds that all such "sightings" can be chalked up to shooting stars, light reflecting off the bellies of geese flying in formation, and the simple misidentification of known aircraft, built by human hands right here on Earth.

Without question, a majority of the sightings of craft like the one Mike and his family observed do involve manmade objects. Though it will certainly arrive with dismay among many in the UFO research community, my gut tells me this about the saucer hovering over that power substation in 1973: Although appearing highly advanced and otherworldly, even my earliest, most peripheral observations regarding the possible mechanics behind its operation suggest strongly that the UFO was made functional by technology that *could exist right here on Earth.* Granted, I can't say with certainty that whatever it was Mike and the others saw that night was indeed manmade. Still, I feel that it is an equal leap of faith—if not perhaps a greater stretch—to assume that it was extraterrestrial, based only on the scant evidence we have available to us. Some kind of human technology seems more likely in this case, although qualifying what exactly we mean by "human" can be difficult, as we've begun to outline already in previous chapters. For instance, could it be that the traditional "UFO encounter" itself merely represents some perceptible aspect of a technology that, in truth, emanates from our own future?

The majority of this book thus far has dealt with attempting to discern clues about the UFO enigma from both clandestine activities that have taken place in the past, as well as from the study of trends we see as we enter the exciting technological age our future represents. At this point, I felt that the in-depth examination of at least one unique case would not only help lend some credibility to a few of the arguments that will be presented later, but also to help dispel a few of the expected complaints and criticisms regarding "armchair researchers." Although it is true that proper, thorough research should involve both fieldwork *and* detailed examination of the available data, with specific regard to the study of UFOs, we are indeed presented with rather unique circumstances—and thus, a number of unique limitations. Chief among these is the fact that, as most serious UFO researchers know already, predicting the appearance of such an extraordinary object is all but impossible. This leaves researchers in an undesirable position of having to wait until a chance encounter has already occurred, and only then can they race to the scene, hoping to scrounge around for evidence of the impossible before it's too late.

Mike Reese at the site of his 1973 Locust Grove UFO encounter.

In the case of Mike Reese, we were nearly four decades too late getting back to the scene of his encounter, although in early 2012, Mike and I did manage to make the drive together back to the infamous power substation where the vivid UFO sighting had occurred back in 1973. The afternoon we arrived to take photos of the area, I could sense that a bit of nostalgia had overtaken Mike as he stood posing for me in front of the location, to which he hadn't returned to visit, even once, in all those years. And even so many decades after the fact, the circumstances underlying our belated return visit still proved to be rather odd, if not slightly humorous. For instance, we noted, as if on cue, the appearance of two large black helicopters passing overhead just as I began to take photos of the area. Mike and I waved at the aircraft as they passed overhead, and joked that, even after all that time, although it seemed unlikely, someone might still be interested in our humble and inquisitive activity in the area.

I do believe the old axiom, however, that states that it is better to be late than to never arrive at all. In the case of Mike's 1973 encounter, his thorough ability to recollect the details of the event would indeed prove to be very useful at a later time. Within just weeks of my publisher's deadline for this book, I happened to be introduced to a young man through a mutual friend who shared yet another vivid UFO sighting he and several others witnessed one evening while traveling abroad through parts of Asia the previous summer. The individual requested that his name, as well as the specific location of the sighting, be omitted from this report, due to the personally disturbing nature of his encounter.

The witness, who we will call "Andy," had been visiting with friends overseas in the summer of 2011. One evening, he and several others were outdoors together, and observed a strange light that had appeared in the distance. As the object moved closer to them, Andy began to make out a triangular shape, with a variety of colored lights that appeared to revolve around the edges of the craft, one after the other, in sequence. The colors, of course, had been red, green, and blue; even so many years later, the significance here in relation to what Mike Reese had described seeing in 1973, is quite obvious.

Andy and his company watched the object for a period that he believed could have been well more than an hour, and although they observed it continuously during this period, never leaving the area where they had been when it first appeared, Andy nonetheless described this event as one of the most frightening experiences of his life. The object drifted more or less slowly overhead for a long while, and had at this point been observed for a long period of time. Then, suddenly, the craft purportedly moved very quickly toward one end of the horizon, only to remove itself just as quickly to the other, beginning an erratic ascent in zigzag fashion, before propelling itself forward in what Andy described as being an absolutely tremendous speed. According to Andy, the craft's line of flight, paired with its speed, gave the appearance that its path had managed to visibly follow the curvature of the Earth itself.

At this point in our discussion, Andy told me that our mutual acquaintance had indeed made him aware of my work in ufology, and that he was mildly concerned about the potential for me writing about this sighting, unless I changed or omitted his name, along with the physical location of the sighting. Given its relevance to the 1973 Locust Grove sighting, I agreed to Andy's terms, so that at least the general details of his story could be included here for sake of comparison between the two reports. What, if anything, might we learn from the curious preponderance of similarities among reports like these, in terms of physical attributes such as the colors revolving around both the UFO craft described in these separate encounters? Could this offer any new clues about the ways such highly advanced aircraft operate?

I also managed to gather a bit of information on Andy's educational background and personal beliefs. He is 25 years old and is a devout Christian, though he described being careful not to seem abrasive or outspoken with his beliefs. Andy studied subjects in college that included biology and quantum physics, and expressed that he is well aware of the incredible nature of the sighting, based on the seemingly erratic flight capabilities of the object he observed. Furthermore, he told me that the object in question had caused him not to want to think about UFOs anymore, or even some areas of the known sciences, because the implications of his encounter had frightened him too badly. When I suggested that, in my opinion, it is at least possible that this object could have been some advanced form of terrestrial technology, Andy disagreed strongly, and based on his observations, believed instead that the craft he witnessed could not possibly have been anything of this Earth.

In the end, we must be willing to consider *all* the vast possibilities that await us in trying to decipher such incredible circumstances, especially those that best cater to increasing our understanding. The various phenomena actually constituting what we use the blanket term *UFO* to describe arrive in many forms; some of these may involve manmade craft, whereas others may be atmospheric anomalies, or even dimensional aberrations that defy our laws of physics. Perhaps in some instances there is even justification for an extraterrestrial origin. But before we draw such conclusions, the best we can hope to do is to attempt to understand the phenomenon to its fullest, achievable only by breaking down the many complex potential varieties of the UFO experience, and not glossing over their entirety with preconceptions that we are, without question, dealing with alien craft from outer space; this simply may not be the case. Based on the evidence provided in eyewitness reports like those of Andy, Mike Reese, and countless others, there may be clues yet to be discovered that will hint at the true nature of some of these strange craft, their different varieties and origins, and, ultimately, their purpose for being.

Perhaps, with some luck, we'll even be afforded a glimpse at how it all relates to our existence here on planet Earth. I suspect, however, that even such a momentary or cursory view of the phenomenon would nonetheless betray it as being far closer to us than we have previously been willing to realize or accept—whether that is simply for perceptual reasons, or out of the stark fear that might emanate from any such bold alternative.

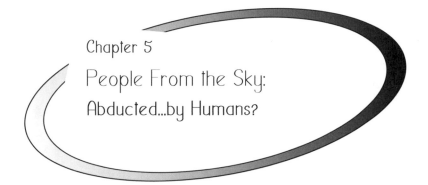

Chapter 5

People From the Sky:
Abducted...by Humans?

*A mind is a terrible thing to waste—and a
worse thing to commandeer.*

—Martin Cannon,
The Controllers

Often in life, our introduction to bold and shattering new ideas can arrive under rather strange circumstances. A fine example of this occurred in 1947, while Dr. Percy LeBaron Spencer had been engaged in the design of magnetrons for radar systems with the Raytheon Company. One afternoon, as he was walking past a radar tube, he found to his surprise that a Mr. Goodbar candy bar he had been carrying in his pocket had melted. Intrigued by this, he then tried exposing popcorn to the microwave radiation emanating from the tube, which began to pop all over the room. To further verify his findings, he designed an experiment where a high-density electromagnetic field was filtered into a metal box using microwaves, from which it had no way to escape. By placing foods within the box, he found that they could be heated very quickly, and thus the microwave oven was born.[1]

I'm making a somewhat whimsical allusion, between the funny conditions under which people are often exposed to new ideas—typically by pure chance or as a result of accidental circumstances—and the ways I've personally stumbled onto certain perceptions of UFO related subjects. Hence, the story I'm about to relate here—involving one of the more curious and clandestine aspects of the

UFO mystery—took place in a pub, of all places, along the border of the North Georgia Highlands. I was having a brief discussion one Wednesday evening in December 2011 with a girl named Amy, one of the locale's regular patrons, when a peculiar clue to the enduring UFO mystery seemed to break free from our otherwise-random exchange.

"What is it you do during the daytime," she asked, sensing that perhaps the life of a professional musician had its innate financial limitations.[2]

"Well, I'm actually a writer during the nine-to-five hours," I explained. Next she asked what sorts of things I chose to write about, to which my typical answer is simply "weird stuff." Maybe if I'm feeling a bit more adventurous at any given moment, I'll go a bit further and refer to it as "culture and philosophy." For those willing to probe even deeper, I might explain that the majority of my research actually deals with UFOs and Forteana, if they appear to *really* be in the know.

"Oh, so you write about aliens abducting people and stuff," she said with an accepting tone. "That's funny, because my dad's mother has said for a long time that she was taken onto a space ship and examined back in the 1970s."

"Interesting," I told her, my intrigue now changing hues slightly. Surprisingly, I hear references to this sort of thing quite often, but the circumstances Amy was about to relate were quite different.

"Yeah, but they say she's a little crazy. And the weird thing about it was that she said that when they took her on board, they did all these tests on her; but they weren't aliens or anything," Amy said, grasping for words a bit. "She said they were people on board that thing."

"Wait—people? You mean *humans?*"

"That's right," Amy said. "She lives in Florida now, but if she's ever in town, I'll try and bring her by to speak to you."

We continued discussing her grandmother's experience, as well as the general subject of alien abduction and, before we parted ways, I passed my card along to her.

"Let me know if you think your grandmother would ever be interested in talking about this," I said. "And you can tell her I'm legit. This won't be appearing in *The National Enquirer.*"

Within just days of being told even the sparsest details about this strange encounter with "humans" aboard an exotic aircraft, one of the listeners of my weekly podcast contacted me to relate another odd UFO incident, which also seemed to deal with humans seen on board a UFO:

Hi Micah,

Ever wonder how many UFO sightings never get talked about? I played banjo in a band up in northern New York State where I was living in 2000. I used to ride with our fiddler to many of the events where the band played and he told me about seeing a UFO back in the 80's near where he lived near Chippewa Bay on the St. Lawrence River. He told me not to tell anyone because he didn't want the ridicule that he started to get when he told a couple of people about it, so I never talked about it to people. He passed away in 2008, so I see no harm in sharing his story now with someone who can appreciate it (I am a listener of The Gralien Report). I have to wonder how many other stories never get shared due to fear of ridicule.

He said that he was driving on Route 37 when he came to the intersection of Triangle Road, which went to Chippewa Bay, when he saw what he thought was a very low-flying airplane over the woods behind an abandoned farmhouse. As he got closer, he noticed that the object was not moving very fast, and actually appeared to be hovering, like a helicopter, over the trees. Curious about it, he slowed down and pulled his pickup truck over to the side of the road. The more he looked at it he began to realize that it didn't look like anything he had ever seen before. He said it looked like a small building with large lit up windows in it, floating in air. He compared its appearance to one of the restaurants in Watertown, NY that had a classic diner theme (stainless steel exterior with large windows). The object floated over the road behind him and he turned his truck around and tried to follow it. He took a couple of side roads and managed to again get close to the object, close enough so that he said he could see people inside as the object got closer to him. He said the people appeared to be dressed like doctors, and there were what looked like stainless steel tables inside. He said that he began to feel uneasy as the object got closer to him, and suddenly he just had to get away from it. He drove away as fast as he could, fearing that it might now be following him. He said that later when he told people about it, they made fun of him and asked what he'd been drinking (or smoking), so he quit talking about it. One of the people he shared the story with said that they saw what looked like a large shooting star on that same evening.[3]

———————

Needless to say, the description of there being "people" on board the UFO craft during the encounter had fascinated me. Still, I surmised that the average witness to circumstances such as those described here might compare any generally anthropomorphic figure that they may have seen to being "people." I responded to the message, asking whether the gentleman who witnessed the craft had noted the shape or rough dimensions of the craft itself, as well as to see if I could get further clarification on the appearance of the "doctors" he had seen through the windows of the craft. This is the reply I received:

———————

My friend really didn't go into great detail about the shape of the craft when I asked about what it looked like. He must have felt comparing it to a local landmark I was familiar with at the time would best convey his description to me. The building he compared it to had been a place called Vinnie Bink's Classic Diner, which has since been torn down, I believe. It was a rectangular building with an "Art Deco" fashioned exterior that had a metallic look and large windows. It kind of does look like what I think a UFO might look like, based on other descriptions and artwork I've seen, although not a strict "saucer" or "triangle" shape.

He did not lead me to think that the figures he saw inside were other than human beings. What he said was, "doctors or people in lab coats." He didn't elaborate on the color of what they were wearing in his description and I didn't press for more detail. I just imagined the green doctor's smocks or white lab coats. I wish I had asked more questions, but he didn't seem comfortable talking any more about it, so I dropped it.

My friend died in '08 at the age of 88 and his wife followed him about a month or two later (odd how that happens).[4]

So far as my contact had been able to discern, the witness had seemed to indicate that the beings on board the craft had been human, or at very least, had appeared as such. Though the circumstances related above already outline the curious "human" aspects that many UFO reports seem to involve, another classic was recounted by Jacques Vallee in his book *Dimensions*, which nonetheless helps to drive the point home. On March 23, 1966, an aircraft electronics instructor had been driving to work at approximately 5 a.m. near Temple, Oklahoma, when he saw a bright light emanating from someplace along the roadway ahead. The light was soon revealed to be coming from a strange object resting on the highway, resembling "an aluminum airliner with no wings or tail and with no seams along the fuselage."[5] Crouched near the object had been a man, described by the witness as "a plain old G.I. mechanic...or a crew chief or whatever he might happen to be on that crew. He had a flashlight in his hand, and he was almost kneeling on his right knee, with his left hand touching the bottom of the fuselage."[6]

This sort of scenario also begins to present itself within a number of different reports of alien abduction that have appeared throughout the years. Consider a few very famous cases, such as the November 5, 1975 abduction of Travis Walton, which we touched on briefly in the Introduction. Indeed, although Walton claimed to have recollection of meeting the fairly prototypical "greys," his more notable interactions on board what he perceived to be an alien craft had involved humanlike beings that were unordinary only in that, to borrow Walton's description, they were the "epitome of their gender."[7] These beings then led him to an area where he was laid on a table, and an item that resembled—to a suspicious degree—an oxygen mask just like an anesthesiologist might use to administer aerosolized or gaseous drugs to a patient. Of course, Walton then blacked out, as might be expected of any man having anesthesia administered. This aspect of his story presents us with a surprisingly common conundrum that reoccurs throughout UFO abduction reports: The "alien" beings on board what are obviously highly advanced aircraft nonetheless utilize rather unsophisticated surgical procedures on the humans they examine. No better example of this exists, perhaps, than Betty and Barney Hill's famous abduction in 1961, during which strangely antiquated tests for pregnancy were allegedly performed on Mrs. Hill.[8] I would not be the first to say that these beings, had they managed to develop technology that brought them all the way from Zeta Reticuli, would likely have also developed less-archaic tests for such things as determining pregnancy.

Despite the wide variety "beings" commonly reported in various UFO literature, the specific appearances of humanlike extraterrestrials had become prevalent enough by the 1980s for them to garner a few specific names, including terms such as "Nordics," "Space Brothers," and the popular title of "Pleiadians," which remains in use today by the UFO Contact Center International.[9] Though some reports of alleged "Nordic" entities describe them as being slightly larger than the average human, they otherwise tend to be remarkably consistent in their resemblance to the average Earth-dweller. All things considered, it is a bit strange that beings appearing to resemble humans so closely are nonetheless categorized alongside different varieties of supposed "extraterrestrials." Perhaps what this really illustrates for us is the insidiousness of the extraterrestrial *meme*, supplanted within the public subconscious early on; whether this was through the intentional use of misinformation, or merely as a result of speculation by a pre-Space Age scientific establishment regarding what UFOs might be, we cannot be certain. The end result, however, is painfully obvious: When the obvious presence of *humans* appears in the recollections of contactees and victims of UFO abduction, they are typically referred to as being merely "humanlike" at very best, though far more often as being aliens from another world—despite what their appearance might otherwise betray about the circumstances.

Humans hard at work de-ionizing a "flying saucer"?

Admittedly, I am not a person who claims to have had interactions with anything that appeared to be an extraterrestrial being in my life, and thus my attempts at humble speculation on the subject of alien abduction and, more specifically, "alternative theories" in that regard do often draw criticism. This is especially the case with individuals who report having had their own encounters. Shortly after an article I wrote on the subject, with regard to the existence of a possible human element present amid some alien abduction and UFO reports, a rather scathing exchange appeared online, a portion of which I've excerpted here:

> I still get sick with worry that (my abduction experiences) can't be real...but why do others with me see the same thing??
>
> Quit this BS theorizing by talking heads who like the attention [they get from] telling scary stories and showing how smart they are by trying to explain it away.[10]

I'm well enough beyond getting incensed these days when such commentary appears to be directed at me; in fact, if anything, I find myself gravitating toward earnest feelings of sympathy for those who claim to have had troubling experiences like this, which neither party— abductee or ufologist—can seem to explain entirely. Indeed, having not "been there" myself, it is difficult to surmise what others who say they have had the intrusive experience of alien abduction occur in their lives must be feeling. Of course, I imagine this is especially the case when a researcher like me comes along and begins asking questions, which may appear to be aimed at contradicting their claims.

And yet, I feel that there may be common ground between the two camps. Although the apparent presence of an extraterrestrial intelligence behind the mystery seems questionable, it would require a significant leap in our assessment of the situation to assume that the abductees are purely imagining their experiences. Researcher Kevin Randle illustrated very similar feelings during a February 2012 appearance on the popular *Paracast* radio program, where he noted his own gut feeling that "the abduction phenomenon has terrestrial explanations, and that there is nothing extraterrestrial about it."[11] Randle also described various discussions he had shared with abduction researcher Kathleen Marden, who is also the niece of Betty Hill, where they seemed to share the opinion that factors such as sleep paralysis could underlie at least a few abduction reports. "Some abductions are explainable that way, but not all of them, so there are other mechanisms operating there. But I see nothing to suggest that there's an extraterrestrial component to it."[12]

Shortly after I authored the aforementioned article regarding the "human factor" that seems apparent within reports of UFO abduction, I was directed to the work of a researcher named Martin Cannon, whose 1990 essay "The Controllers: A New Hypothesis of Alien Abductions" represents one of the most thorough alternative hypotheses available within the UFO literature regarding abduction research. Cannon's approach deals less with reports of actual UFO craft, and instead focuses on parallels that exist between common aspects of reported alien abductions and intelligence programs involving mind control. "The myth of the UFO has provided an effective cover story for an entirely different sort of mystery," Cannon notes.[13] By removing the warring diametric elements of the "believer" versus "skeptic" mentalities, Cannon believed he had indeed uncovered some aspect of truth surrounding the strange (and at times seemingly *absurd*) stories that comprise the realm of alien abduction. As one might already expect, Cannon's emerging hypothesis has little to do with aliens from outer space; it would, however, incorporate things we might expect from a highly advanced form of "behind the scenes" technology—akin in many ways to that which the Singularitarians might ascribe—and perhaps several decades ahead of mainstream science today. Still, although it fits the scope of this discussion quite neatly, it may be surprising nonetheless to assume that such technology could also be one that is likely of terrestrial origin.

"Both Believer and Skeptic," Cannon writes, "miss the real story. Both make the same mistake: They connect the abduction phenomenon to the forty-year history of UFO sightings, and they apply their prejudices about the latter to the controversy about the former."[14] As researchers, when we begin to remove some of the preconceptions and stop overlooking the stranger, often more revealing elements tucked away within the UFO mystery, at least some of the accounts of alien abduction become more plausible. In many instances, they also betray a number of quirky details that seem entirely inconsistent with the idea of an advanced extraterrestrial race with knowledge that exceeds our own. As noted here, and several times already in this chapter, also central to Cannon's argument is the fact that UFO abductors, which are often presumed to be "alien," seem to use technology that is startlingly underwhelming in its sophistication:

> Why—if we take UFO abduction accounts at face value—are the "advanced aliens" using an old technology, an Earth technology, a technology that may soon be rendered obsolescent, if it hasn't been so rendered already? I am reminded of the charming anachronisms in the old Flash Gordon serials, where swords and spaceships clashed continually.
>
> Do they also watch black-and-white television on Zeta Reticuli?[15]

To be specific, the sorts of "obsolete" technologies to which Cannon refers are perhaps best represented in the antiquated methods of testing for pregnancy that abductees claim to have undergone, much like the circumstances described by abductee Betty Hill during her 1961 encounter. It should be noted, of course, that the amniocentesis procedures Hill seemed to describe *were* indeed quite advanced at the time of her encounter. Cannon, however, takes issue with the assertion that this represented a highly advanced alien race:

> Some ufologists rashly assume that Betty Hill's "pregnancy test" is evidence of advanced

extraterrestrial technology, since her 1961 account pre-dates the official announcement of amniocentesis, which does indeed make use of a needle inserted into the navel. But we now have much less invasive means of testing for pregnancy than amniocentesis. True, amniocentesis is still sometimes used to gather information about the fetus, but the wielders of a highly evolved technology would certainly use other methods of determining the existence of pregnancy in the first place.[16]

Seemingly in contrast to this, other varieties of technology begin to surface that *do* seem, at least superficially, to be more advanced in nature. Consider, for instance, the stories of alleged "implants" recovered from various places within the bodies of the abductees that include the nasal passage and, in more extreme cases, even from directly within the skull. Sometimes these foreign objects are located in conjunction with a small scar, typically described as resembling a "scoop mark" or series of similar markings on the skin; in other instances, foreign-looking bits of metal and other substances appear in the complete absence of any external scarring at all. The latter circumstance has especially contributed to the presumption that the alleged "alien implants" are being inserted by individuals with technology so advanced that they can do so without leaving any evidence of surgical intrusion whatsoever. We might consider, however, the steady advances seen with every passing year regarding varieties of minimally invasive surgeries; in addition to such procedures as laparoscopy performed in the abdominal region, think for a moment how well plastic surgeons are getting at covering their tracks, especially when the surgeries involved are for cosmetic reasons, aimed at improving the appearance of various parts of the body! And there still could be far more natural explanations underlying a few of the alleged "implants," if we stop to consider medical conditions like channelopathies and ion channel mutations, which might in some cases contribute to the appearances of seemingly "foreign" deposits of minerals and other substances taken into our bodies in small amounts as we digest the foods we eat.

If nothing else, we can begin to recognize that even the seemingly foreign implants found within the bodies of some claiming to have undergone abductions could have underlying prosaic causes. But the point here is not to dismiss or attack the claims of the abductees themselves. Quite the contrary, our discussion of potential causes behind such things as implanted probes and other physical objects found within parts of the body will help to *substantiate* those claims. After all, Occam's Razor might again be invoked with the assumption that implanting such objects within the human body *must* be the work of a highly advanced form of technology. However, this becomes quite unlikely (or outright impossible) in the event that Earth is *not* undergoing visitation by advanced extraterrestrials. On the other hand, if we had proof that the technologies in use during such clandestine surgeries were indeed quite easily attained in the here-and-now, the claims of the abductees might not seem so "out of this world" after all—and hence also may be far more accurate and rooted in truth than most realize.

Cannon goes on to note a discourse that took place in 1953 between the Director of the National Institute of Mental Health and sensory deprivation researcher John C. Lilly, as recounted in Lilly's biography. Lilly was apparently asked "to brief the CIA, FBI, NSA and the various military intelligence services on his work using electrodes to stimulate directly the pleasure and pain centers of the brain."[17] Lilly seemed to indicate non-compliance with this request, noting that his associate, Dr. Antoine Remond

> [h]as demonstrated that this method of stimulation of the brain can be applied to the human without the help of the neurosurgeon; he is doing it in his office in Paris without neurosurgical supervision. This means that anybody with the proper apparatus can carry this out on a person covertly, with no external signs that electrodes have been used on that person.[18]

Keep in mind, again, that although this may sound far less interesting (or relevant) to us in the 21st century, the processes being described here were already taking place in Paris *as far back as 1953* (and thus, the reader is encouraged here to imagine what other similar sorts of technology might have been in use already by 1953, or even a decade later, by which time the famous Hill abduction incident had already taken place). Lilly went on to note: "I feel that if this technique got into the hands of a secret agency, they would have total control over a human being and be able to change his beliefs extremely quickly, leaving little evidence of what they had done."[19]

Although the above circumstances being related have to do with the potentials for such technology being harnessed by covert agencies, there are other ways that advances in the sciences might be used to control or manipulate an individual. Cannon points out that, much as we discerned earlier with regard to advanced "airships" that may have been under construction covertly by the end of the 19th century, military interests aren't always the only medium through which the advancement of secret technology can occur:

There are important elements in the scientific community, powerful people, who are very much interested in these areas...but they have to keep most of their work secret. Because as soon as they start to publish some of these sensitive things, they have problems in their lives. You see, they work on research grants, and if you follow the research being done, you find that as soon as these scientists publish something about this, their research funds are cut off. There are areas in bioelectric research where very simple techniques and devices can have mind-boggling effects. Conceivably, if you have a crazed person with a bit of a technical background, he can do a lot of damage.[20]

Again, this is supposing that such research is taking place as a result of *private interests*, and largely away from public perception. In the event that such technology does eventually fall under the observation of government agencies, we can see that it would no doubt *remain* clandestine.

So why do we bring all this to the table here, if not to try and dispel the mythos surrounding what many perceive as the phenomenon known as "alien abduction"? The information presented here begins to show us that, in addition to affirmation that government agencies are often working with technology a few decades ahead of that which the public is made aware, this sort of technology could, rather obviously, be implemented on a population in covert ways, aimed at achieving various methods of control, misdirection, and other not-so-savory purposes. And to further justify such assumptions, a large swathe of the *known* research by government agencies into areas involving mind control, hypnosis, and covertly monitoring individuals has been made public knowledge, as a result of Senate hearings on CIA projects that include infamous names including MKULTRA, among others.[21] Orwell might indeed be rolling over in his grave at the very thought of such gross overreaches of power amid various government agencies; what's even worse is that a strong likelihood remains that such practices may have continued well beyond the MKULTRA years, and have done so, at least in part, beneath the Fabian façade of a nonhuman, extraterrestrial presence in our midst.

In short, if the abductees are correct, they've been made unwilling recipients of *some* variety of control and manipulation, with the strong likelihood that they were all the while being misled to think their interactions were otherworldly. Hence, the victims of such encounters are made out to seem like crazy buffoons, ceding to the ails of an overactive imagination, or an unstable lust for involvement with matters not entirely of this world. When viewed in this way, aspects of the alien abduction enigma can even become tragic, in a sense. And of course, at the end of the day we're still no closer to cracking the great cosmic egg that contains the golden heart of the UFO mystery.

Or are we?

Perhaps there are a few things we can surmise from this scenario after all. The supposition that there may be a terrestrial, anthropocentric element to the abduction phenomenon would entail that there is indeed an entire host of advanced technologies working covertly to orchestrate the appearance of an enigmatic, extraterrestrial presence. Such things as amniocentesis in the Betty and Barney Hill abduction might suggest that, rather than being the work of aliens that are potentially *several thousands* of years more advanced than we, we are seeing a technology that was perhaps within just a few years of that in common use by 1961. Thus, supposing that the suppression of certain discoveries might further contribute to the appearance of seemingly "exotic" technologies, we are again confronted with the possibility that human organizations might be involved. Additionally, we must consider that if they are in the neighborhood of being one or two decades "ahead of the curve," so to speak, today that would place them in the same ballpark of approaching near-Singularity technologies.

That is, of course, if Kurzweil and the others of his futurologist ilk are right about their projected arrival of the so-called *knee of the curve*. This term references the period where humanity is expected begin its rapid, greater-than-exponential ascent toward technological hyper-development, which will precede the emergence of artificial intelligence that matches or exceeds human abilities and, ultimately, the event we call the Singularity. But if the Singularitarians aren't taking into consideration what clandestine technologies might be in use *behind the scenes* already, it stands to reason that humanity could actually be far closer to reaching Singularity than the majority of us are aware of. Again, to borrow Kurzweil's own words, the Singularity could be very near, indeed.

In this context, the apparent presence of alien abduction offers just one more avenue by which we are made potentially aware that the "UFO enigma" could have been exploited, to some degree, for purposes of masking more highly advanced technologies right here in ours midst. And yet, although some (or even all) abduction hypotheses might be explainable along the lines of underlying Earth-based projects and organizations, it still seems that there may be *something more* going on here—something beyond what most in the mainstream sciences, or even certain areas of officialdom, are aware of or willing to consider.

In previous chapters, I've touched on the possibility that at least certain aspects of the broader UFO mystery could constitute a form of technology emanating from our own future. Conceivably, this might also exist without the presence of a literal "time traveling" apparatus as depicted (often whimsically, and in romantic fashion) in popular fiction. It is beyond the scope of the present argument to speculate as to precisely how this might occur, though later we will revisit the idea and its implications more in depth. For the time being, however, so as to be sure and take all possible variables into consideration, we will turn our attention again toward the potentials for alien life that may exist elsewhere in the universe, and what potentials such a technological presence may yield. Arguably, whether it be the case that UFOs are evidence of time travelers from our own future, secret earthbound technologies being used by our world governments or—as we're about to consider more fully—literal alien beings from other worlds, there is hardly a better place to look for evidence of what future science may yield than in the wake of these strange and enigmatic UFO visitors that, at least seemingly, arrive here from the heavens.

No matter what their true origin may be, we nonetheless must accept the likelihood that UFOs and their associated technologies will likely prove to represent some form of what we could call *near-* or even *post-Singularity* intelligence. And in the event that they *are* actually extraterrestrial beings traveling here from other worlds, there simply may be no other alternative that could effectively explain all the awesome, seemingly impossible feats they achieve—things that previous authors on this subject have already chronicled admirably, with purposeful, determined, and unwavering consistency.

Though it hardly requires any mention here, I sense that I fall short of qualifying among the ranks of such chroniclers. With any luck, however, my present treatise on this great and enduring mystery will nonetheless be viewed in hindsight by future generations as a successful thought experiment, set forth by a man with his own resolute and rather atypical sense of discernment. Hopefully, in retrospect, it will also be one that managed to yield certain results. As I suspect that even the man of some distant future epoch will at some point find himself saying, *only time will tell.*

"Humans From the Sky." Artwork by Caleb Hanks.

Chapter 6

Transcendent Biology:
The Science of Alien Visitation

*Within twenty five years our own biological
science will be able to reliably alter the
genetic characteristics of human beings.
We will create enhanced humans adapted
to special conditions, such as life in
outer space. Wouldn't we expect the UFO
occupants to do the same, rather than
adopting the human shape which is far
from representing the biological optimum?*
—Dr. Jacques Vallee,
Dimensions: A Casebook of Alien Contact

Throughout the last several decades, a number of well-respected scientific minds have come and gone, grappling amid footholds along the slippery slope that constitutes modern ufology. James E. McDonald, noted meteorology professor and senior physicist at the Institute for Atmospheric Physics, was no exception to this intrepid bunch. In 1969, he presented a report to the American Association for the Advancement of Science, where he leveled his feelings behind the reasonable advocacy for there being an extraterrestrial component underlying some UFO reports. McDonald advised:

> Present evidence surely does not amount to incontrovertible proof of the extraterrestrial hypothesis. What I find scientifically dismaying is that, while a large body of UFO evidence now seems to point in no other direction than the extraterrestrial hypothesis, the profoundly important implications of that possibility are going unconsidered by the scientific community because this entire problem has been imputed to be little more than a nonsense matter unworthy of serious scientific attention.[1]

McDonald had no doubt been directing this complaint, at least in part, at the infamous University of Colorado UFO Project, better known as the Condon Committee, which had effectively shredded any air of respectability UFOs may have maintained in the eyes of the scientific community at large during the late 1960s. Despite the façade of "science" supposedly underlying the entire affair, history shows that the Condon Committee, which *did* end up having a tremendous influence on the way UFOs were perceived by official institutions in the years that followed, had been guilty of a number of gross preconceptions by its members. A fine example of this had become public knowledge by as early as February 1967, when Edward Condon was quoted by the Elmira, New York, *Star-Gazette* during a speaking engagement stating that his "attitude right now is that there's nothing to (UFOs), but I'm not supposed to reach a conclusion for another year."[2]

This was further compounded by later revelations that Robert J. Low, the Condon Committee's project coordinator, had argued early on that the subversive use of misdirection and carefully orchestrated deception of the public with the Committee's "investigation" might be beneficial. To borrow Low's own words, which appeared in a memo he authored on August 9, 1966, titled "Some Thoughts on the UFO Project": "The trick would be, I think, to describe the project so that, to the public, it would appear a totally objective study but, to the scientific community, would present the image of a group of nonbelievers trying their best to be objective, but having almost zero expectation of finding a saucer."[3]

This so-called "trick," as outlined by Mr. Low, was obviously self-serving—or, at the very least, aimed at serving *somebody's* ulterior motives—as was indicated later in the same memorandum: "I'm inclined to feel at this early stage that, if we set up the thing right and take pains to get the proper people involved and have success in presenting the image we want to present to the scientific community, we could carry the job off to our benefit."[4]

So disheartening were Low's words, illuminating the intended purpose of the Condon Committee as a vehicle for widespread deception, rather than one for unbiased scientific inquiry, that the late Arthur Koestler wrote of the affair that

> [t]he Low memorandum can only be viewed as a deliberate act calculated to deceive; to deceive first the scientific community, and, through them, the public at large. I know of no modern parallel to such a cynical act of duplicity on the part of a university official.... By the writing of such a document, the integrity of the entire project was shattered in advance.[5]

Despite the grossly unscientific hijinks that can be directly attributed to the Condon Committee and their "analysis" of the UFO mystery, the scope of the present argument is not to try to lift the frayed remains of a plausible extraterrestrial hypothesis for UFO activity from the proverbial ashes. Nor does this author, in fact, advocate the idea that the UFO problem can be entirely constituted by any singular, wild theory such as aliens visiting from space (or any other sole, all-inclusive explanation one may hope to present for the phenomenon). However, with regard to technological Singularity, a number of concepts are worthy of being addressed here when it comes to the potential for alien life existing elsewhere in the universe, and to date it seems there is very little—if any—honest dialogue underway where the participants are willing to addresses such things. The guilt lies not just among the Transhumanist thinkers, but also their cousins among the UFO community. I'm certain that, by referring to these two camps as "cousins," I have elicited a few cringes already. However, should this dialogue I propose ever truly be allowed to begin, I suspect that the differences between these two seemingly disparate schools of study would be rendered fewer in number than most would expect.

A few key points need to be addressed here right off the bat. Namely, if Kurzweil and his fellow Singularitarians are correct in their estimates with regard to technological advances that will occur here on Earth throughout the next several decades, it is curious, then, that some alien race has not achieved these already—or have they? However primitive our species might be in comparison to an alien race that came to visit us, in the event that some advanced society *had* undergone a Singularity similar to that which Transhumanists forecast for the coming decades, we likely would still be capable of perceiving at least a few limited aspects of this technology and its presence. Perhaps this could occur even in lieu of facing the burden of traveling all the way to Earth for ongoing visitation; this would especially be the case if they *did* use their technology to begin exploring and colonizing distant regions of space (which, to no one's particular surprise, is something that is often incorporated into the mythos surrounding different interpretations of eventual Transhumanism, as well as extraterrestrial life). Thus, we are left to ponder a few different alternatives:

1. Today, although we cannot rule out the possibility of extraterrestrial life existing elsewhere in the Universe, there is still very little verifiable scientific evidence that shows us proof of alien beings visiting Earth. This fundamental viewpoint has been shared by a number of credited and credentialed UFO researchers throughout the years, including the likes of J. Allen Hynek and Jacques Vallee. In other words, *we cannot cite any existing proof that directly correlates UFOs and their activity with a presumed extraterrestrial intelligence.* With the lack of evidence for extraterrestrial activity occurring close enough to be observed by us, we could assume that the Singularitarian view may be essentially wrong, or perhaps severely limited, when applied to how an alien race might progress through their own stages of technological advancement. In essence, we assume that the methods and expected rate of progress among an alien civilization, as well as the various environmental influences on this progress that an alien world

might present, would occur on a basis that is similar or identical to our own (thus we evoke aspects of Brandon Carter's *Anthropic Principle*). If a valid conundrum *did no*t arise from the logical fallacies presented here, then we would not be burdened by such absence of evidence for extraterrestrials, in the midst of otherwise valid phenomenon such as the UFO problem.

2. Alternatively, reports of UFO craft may indeed represent a post-Singularity form of technology that is visiting Earth, and despite the lack of scientific "proof" for the extraterrestrial connection, my earlier assessment that at least *certain* aspects of this supposed technology could be recognized as such by humans would be vindicated. Case in point, the wealth of data already obtained regarding UFO craft and their mysterious activities, though often dismissed by the scientific community, could nonetheless constitute evidence of a technology that is far more advanced than our own. This also brings to mind the notion that a highly advanced alien technology could easily remain partially, or even wholly invisible to us, and perhaps largely due to a sheer lack of interest in establishing "contact" with our species (more on this a bit later) .

3. Finally, there simply may be no advanced civilizations other than our own in existence; or if there are, humanity must be the most highly advanced among them at present, and hence

we see no overt evidence of advanced forms of technology that exist elsewhere in the universe. This is perhaps the *least likely* potential with regard to understanding extraterrestrials and presumed processes of evolution, scientific advancement, colonization, and eventual contact with other intelligent civilizations. This would also imply that all observable UFO phenomena must be either of terrestrial origin, or perhaps some variety of inter- dimensional phenomena.

The prolific reader of available UFO literature will no doubt also take into consideration such things as shadow government cover-ups, efforts to conceal and suppress certain technology, and other conspiracy theories that, if they are true, might hinder or impede access to the *whole truth* behind UFOs. These, of course, are all as worthy of serious consideration as any theory regarding extraterrestrials and their possible origins; however, because by their nature these would involve secrecy, the result would be the obvious ignorance on part of individuals like you or me with regard to exactly what kinds of information may have effectively been concealed. Hence, I've omitted the conspiracy angle here, working on the assumption that we are left to reason primarily with whatever information relating to UFOs we *do* have full access to at present.

Coming back to the second point expressed in my preceding series of possibilities, there is the realistic potential that any highly advanced technology, exceeding our own by hundreds or thousands of years, might be capable of operating in ways that would fall well outside the limitations of what humans can perceive. Carl Sagan, speaking before the Communication with Extraterrestrial Intelligence (CETI) Congress in 1971, summarized the issue thusly:

> We have only to consider the changes in mankind in the last 10^4 years and the potential difficulties which our Pleistocene ancestors would have in accommodation to our present society to realize what an unfathomable gap 10^8 to 10^{10} years represents, even with a tiny rate of intellectual advance. Such societies will have discovered laws of nature and invented technologies whose applications will appear to us indistinguishable from magic. There is a serious question about whether such societies are concerned with communicating with us, any more than we are concerned with communicating with our protozoan or bacterial forebears. We may study microorganisms, but we do not usually communicate with them. I therefore raise the possibility that a horizon in communications interest exists in the evolution of technological societies, and that a civilization very much more advanced than we will be engaged in a busy communications traffic with its peers; but not with us, and not via technologies accessible to us. We may be like the inhabitants of the valleys of New Guinea who may communicate by runner or drum, but who are ignorant of the vast international radio and cable traffic passing over, around and through them.[6]

Indeed, Sagan felt that extraterrestrial communication may likely occur on a level of advancement that would be largely imperceptible to humans. Speculating further, we might surmise that there is an entire host of different activities ET could choose to engage in, which nonetheless may be taking place all around us in the invisible realm that extends beyond the reach of what humans can perceive.

In addition to his theories about the perceptible realms of communication available between humans and other intelligent civilizations, Sagan was also a proponent of the famous Drake Equation, which addresses the likelihood for existence of advanced alien races elsewhere in our universe. Professor Frank Drake proposed the model for this in 1961, around the same time that would serve as the genesis for the ongoing SETI (Search for Extraterrestrial Intelligence) programs of today, having utilized principles of radio astronomy with the intention of contacting other civilizations like our own. Sagan often referenced Drake's Equation in his various books and television appearances, where he used it as a plausible model applied to the search for intelligent alien life.[7] There are, however, at least a few problems with the Drake Equation and the limitations it implies with regard to how life might advance and grow into a technological civilization on a distant planet. For instance, the Drake Equation supposes that many civilizations (if not a majority of them) would potentially destroy themselves once they become technologically proficient, through the use of such things as nuclear weaponry. This reflects, perhaps, the eminent concern over mutually assured destruction that existed during the Cold War years, something that also became key to Sagan's ideology at the time. But taking into consideration the varieties of life forms that might come to exist, especially in distant parts of the known universe, would there not be a potential for vast differences in the ways such an alien species would think and operate? By projecting our inherent humanity into the equation, we might be overlooking a number of circumstances that could prevent the sorts of ordeals and issues that have become paramount to our survival here on Earth.

For instance, consider an advanced race of insects— or at very least, beings that would appear insect-like to you or me—that have evolved to a point of technological proficiency that greatly exceeds our own. Growing and adapting to a planet in a distant star system, these beings might have developed specific attributes fitted to their environment that we would consider very alien indeed. For the sake of example, let's suppose that through time they managed to develop a sort of "hive mentality," similar to the theories of psychologist Carl Jung that involve a collective consciousness that humans subconsciously share. Aliens with similar underlying conscious unity, though obviously to a far greater degree than any that humans may possess, might go about sustaining their civilization with very different moral standards and priorities than we would, on account of this shared form of consciousness.

Remember: This concept is not unlike the ways that some insect species here on Earth are known to operate. We see species such as ants that, rather than being concerned with self-preservation, tend to work collectively in an intricate operation that exists as a variety of miniature elements, culminating to form one standalone, synchronous presence within their humble little anthill. With this in mind, could similar standards of evolutionary operation cause our present, slightly idealistic species of "insect aliens" to work toward preserving its race in strange ways—and at all costs? Also, if this were the case, the notion of mutually assured destruction, which had been so paramount within the context of Drake's Equation, might now seem less likely. We nonetheless might assume that our insectoid neighbors would find it suitable to do such things as attack and destroy another civilization such as ours, as long as doing so benefited their own long-term survival. Again, that hive mentality would seem to prevail strongly.

Taking this a few steps further, what other kinds of biological factors might cause differences in the way a species evolved on distant planets, specifically with regard to their eventual development of intelligence, morals, society, and culture? Would we expect a species of intelligent reptiles—or at least a life form similar to reptiles, as we know them on Earth—to behave differently than evolved mammals such as humans? If so, in what ways would we expect their behavior to differ, based on what we know of reptiles we have interacted with? Would they be more prone to violence and conflict with others, and if so, would this present a threat to their galactic neighbors? Or, would Drake's and Sagan's conclusions be correct in this instance, in that an inherently violent race of reptilian aliens would be less likely to harness advanced technology in the long run on account of their own self-destructive potential?

Then there is the question regarding the physical size of intelligent alien life forms. Could intelligent aliens exist that are diminutive—perhaps only a few micrometers tall, or smaller—but still possessing complex intelligence and the ability to manipulate mass around them in ways that allow them to master their environment? Should we consider whether technology and its applications are typically relative to the physical size and characteristics of the species that harnesses them? And what if a species that was far smaller than humans in stature, but more advanced than we, managed to harness advantages or disadvantages over us with regard to, for instance, a hostile takeover or colonization attempt here on Earth? Alternatively, what about a species so large that their physical presence alongside our own would liken humans to the size of a common field mouse? Though the existence of a creature so large may be impossible on a planet such as Earth, with the amount of gravity our planet exerts on the life forms that populate it, such restrictions may not apply on distant alien worlds.

With that in mind, let's go ahead and consider how environmental factors such as these might affect creatures in different ways from one planet to the next. We are again faced with the notion that various intelligent species, and the physical attributes they would have developed through time, might cause them great difficulty in terms of being equipped for travel to other worlds. The giant I alluded to in the last paragraph, evolving on a planet far smaller than Earth where the demands of gravity on his physical body had been greatly reduced, may find it troubling indeed to visit a planet like ours, where his tremendous musculature would become virtually immovable.

Playing devil's advocate, when we question things such as the physical size of alien beings, perhaps there are certain universal constants that would warrant a few predictable qualities aliens might have instead. For instance, what if the size of quantum particles in the universe acted as a sort of constant, and thus became conducive to—if not an entirely determinant factor in—shaping the size of creatures such as humanoids or other beings with an aptitude for intelligence? This would likely also be relative to the size of a planet where such physical life had appeared, and the resultant gravitational and other physical conditions acting on life as it evolved. In this sense, the evolution of certain intelligent species may indeed be reliant on a fixed set of criteria, in which physical conditions must be met in order for a civilization to evolve in relation to their environment that would lead to advanced intelligence.

And yet, guesswork such as this, regarding the conditions and varieties of alien life elsewhere in our universe, need not be entirely accurate in order to illuminate the tragically anthropomorphic ideals we force onto our galactic neighbors. Our general notion of what may constitute alien life is plagued by projections of our own attributes and the limitations of our human conditioning. Spotting an alien life form, once we restrict them to the rigid confines of being physically "like us," may in the end become virtually impossible. Along with our tendency to presuppose that aliens will bear humanlike traits, there is yet another fundamental flaw with all such presumptions regarding the evolution of an advanced race elsewhere in the universe: All the scenarios set forth up to this point have been contingent on there being a *physical location* (that is, a planet) upon which our presumed aliens would appear and evolve. But how likely is it that there could be other ways intelligent alien life might come to exist in our universe?

Researcher Jay Alfred, citing research by NASA into the potential for what would essentially constitute plasma- based life, discussed in his article "Plasma Life Forms: Dark Panspermia" what other kinds of life might be in existence in various regions of space. Presumably, energetic beings of the variety Alfred describes could also remain largely undetected by us, due to the limitations of human perception and a general lack of scientific instrumentation required for their observation:

> Weird life may not only be "out there"...but it may very well be in your living room. NASA's astrobiology team would need to categorize the life forms that have been described as ghosts, angels and

deities as weird plasma-based life forms and study them within a scientific framework to the extent allowed by current technology. Any confirmation of their existence would revolutionize our understanding of the scope of evolution at many different levels of existence, not just the biochemical level.[8]

It is not beyond the realm of possibility that such energetic forms might, by all accounts, constitute a sort of life *not as we know it,* and that they might even be able to exist in the absence of a planetary atmosphere. For all we know, perhaps such entities could rise into existence within the otherwise-uninhabitable extremities of the vacuum. And yet, although speculation of this sort *does* help to broaden our concept of alien life that could populate the broad and empty spacescapes resting between galaxies, their presence alone does little to aid in helping formulate a model for how alien beings might arrive here on Earth. In other words, if we were to suppose for now that even a *fraction* of known UFO reports have to do with some sort of extraterrestrial intelligence, we're left with tackling the manner in which they arrived and the technology that could have allowed it.

One of the most often-cited arguments against the extraterrestrial hypothesis has to do with the fact that space travel, especially on the scale necessary to reach the nearest populated star systems, would be impossible for physical beings such as you or me. We would likely be incapable of reaching such locations within a single lifetime, at least in the absence of propulsions systems that carried us through space at light speed or better. Here we find certain issues begin to arise, just as well; traveling through space at such tremendous speed would put any physical body within the spacecraft in question at the mercy of g-forces and other strains, which it is believed that no living body could endure. So even in the event that speeds could be attained that would allow for travel to a distant star system within a single lifetime, the stress this would impose on a living body might nonetheless render such travel impossible.

This would be the case, of course, unless *the physical bodies in question were modified and improved in some manner*, which might allow them to become better suited for space travel. This, as I referenced earlier, is reminiscent of the characters portrayed in popular fiction such as the *Transformers*, in which Optimus Prime and the Autobots represent some form of sentient intelligence, but one that is mechanical, rather than organic in nature. Furthermore, they are—and have *always* been, as far as they know—robotic in nature, rather than being the result of cybernetic modifications that supplemented (or even replaced altogether) some kind of organic physical body.

In Transhumanism, we see many similar themes begin to emerge. In addition to the potential for cybernetic modification of a physical body to improve one's natural abilities, we also see the creation of artificial intelligence that is wholly autonomous and in the absence of any underlying organic entity. In keeping with the varieties of modified or entirely artificial beings that Transhumanist thinkers have envisioned for our own future, there are perhaps a handful of UFO researchers today who have surmised how some instances of unexplained aerial phenomena (UAP) might also represent some kind of robotic intelligence. Even going as far back as the Project Bluebook years, a few accredited scientists had questioned whether UFO craft might be something akin to robotic "drones" that were dropped into our atmosphere by a larger mother ship, which rested well outside Earth's atmosphere.[9] But the underlying theme here is centered on the advantages any intelligence that had undergone vast technological enhancement might retain. Indeed, they might become far better suited for the sorts of seemingly impossible tasks we often associate with space travel, in the absence of having physical bodies the likes of which you or I would know. Beings so advanced might not only be physically suited for space travel themselves, but they could also very well harness technologies that would limit the strains which space travel at tremendous speeds might impose on a group of interstellar travelers.

Beings such as these may have even divorced themselves from the necessity for having bodies at all, favoring instead a variety of "psychic embodiment" that frees them from having any physical and intellectual confines. The philosophical study of *embodied cognition* presents us with the concept that the physical form of the human body largely determines the human mind and its processes.

What kinds of thoughts and motivations would drive an intelligence that transcended physicality altogether, having essentially attained a higher form of immortality? It might not be illogical to assume, given these criteria, that the attainment of some form of immortality could even be a requisite for intergalactic space travel and colonization.

As this discussion indicates, the rapid advancement and concurrent physical changes a civilization might go through following technological Singularity, let alone decades and decades of further advancement following the singular point itself, would vastly change the attitudes, motives, and even the innate form of such a race of beings. Having not yet reached this point ourselves, humanity still operates in a veritable Stone Age, in which we have barely harnessed rudiments beyond crude wheels and the sparring use of fire. And yet, we've managed to convince ourselves that simple tools along these lines would still be in use by entities elsewhere in the universe, whose technology instead should far exceed our own. Thus, our search for alien life up to this point has remained void of the proper logical guesswork needed to ascertain what forms, mediums, and motives any highly advanced intelligence might utilize, having undergone technological changes that exceed our own by *at least* several centuries—though probably much more than this.

I feel, in all reverence, that perhaps at this time I should indeed point out that I am by no means the first to have ever conceived of such cosmic variety as what I posit here. A fine (and far earlier) example was afforded us by none other than Howard Phillips Lovecraft, the famous writer of weird fiction, during the early part of the last century. Lovecraft had surmised that the varieties of life on alien worlds

> would deal with beings organized very differently from mundane mammalia, and obeying motives wholly alien to anything we know upon Earth... whether laid in the solar system, or the *utterly unplumbed* gulfs still farther out—the nameless vortices of never-dreamed-of strangeness, where form and symmetry, light and heat, even matter and energy themselves, may be unthinkably metamorphosed or totally wanting.[10]

To speak of the *unthinkable*, there is also the conundrum we could assume with regard to how, without reference to anything similar, the human mind might even attempt to reconcile with intelligence so advanced and different from our own. Let's think, for a moment, back to times far earlier than our own. Had our Cro-Magnon ancestors ever witnessed an SR-71 Blackbird in flight, breaking the sound barrier as it cruised through the sky high above, they likely would have assumed this object to be some great and mighty bird, whose godlike presence brought the sound of thunder with every beating of its wings against the air. The presence of such a magnificent animal, although perhaps rendered a deity on account of its abilities, would nonetheless be grouped alongside various natural phenomena that were known to the ancient mind. In the absence of any better explanation or further ability to observe this strange bird, its presence would be largely accepted as merely being a part of life, exemplified by some variety of phenomena that could not be fully understood. All this might indeed have been the case, of course, only in the event that ancient humans had harnessed the capacity for thought necessary to even *perceive* such phenomenon. For all we know, the complex circumstances an SR-71 Blackbird in flight might have presented to the Cro-Magnon brain would have rendered it virtually *invisible.*

SR-71 Jet.

When we stop to think about the variety of unexplained "natural phenomena" we encounter in our pursuit of knowledge, perhaps we should also consider the likely determinations our ancestors would have made about an advanced technology in their midst. It would be interesting, to say the least, if we learned that much of the natural world around us, and throughout the greater cosmos, were actually the result of such things as fingers on hands that were infinitely more advanced than ours, poking at the stars and planets in orbit. Even more simply, it could be that our apparent ability to sense such subtle things as "winds of change" were the mere result of great and billowing breaths cast from afar, blown in our direction by cosmic lungs that rest well past the edges of time.

Chapter 7

Maleficium Intraspiritus:
Dawn of the Soul Hackers

*Beacons could exist in many modes and for
many differing applications. All who study
extraterrestrial phenomena should be alert
to the possibilities, regardless of the portion
of spectrum of immediate interest to them.*

—Charles L. Seeger,
SETI Program Office,
Ames Research Center, 1977

Imagine a distant future replete with starships, robotic intelligences, and advanced machines—the likes of which most of us know already courtesy of science fiction stories and films—in which humans populate the entire galaxy. There, in some far-off and distant region of space, where perils and threats must inevitably await those brave enough to plunge into their depths, an unknown enemy has intercepted a manned, unidentified starship. This newly discovered threat is both deadly and inhuman—a formidable hunter designed by a civilization long extinct, and for the mere purpose of destroying all varieties of life it comes across with extreme prejudice.

Hidden aboard his Fortress Ship, a lone individual has assessed this dangerous new enemy and is trapped amid demanding circumstances. He must conceive of a way to fool this deadly machine, which seeks to find the presence of conscious life aboard the spaceship it has discovered. The only way the killer outside may be evaded is through a complex and demanding trick: Our protagonist must escape by *simulating* another kind of intelligence— perhaps one that is artificial in nature—which resides aboard the vessel in his stead.

The scenario I've outlined here is quite similar to one that appeared in the 1963 short story "Without a

Thought," which became the first in a long lineage of tales by author Fred Saberhagen involving a horrific machine intelligence known as the Berserkers. Saberhagen's famous creations were a kind of robotic intelligence, capable of self-replication, that were initially designed by a race known as the Builders for purposes of warfare against the Red Race, their rival civilization. The Berserkers were ultimately successful in wiping out the Builders' enemies, but despite this victory, a subsequent malfunction caused the Berserkers to turn on their creators, destroy them, and eventually pursue the destruction of all known life forms elsewhere in the universe.

We often take for granted the idea that alien beings, with the technological advances required of a civilization in order to traverse the cosmos, would be benevolent and caring toward humankind. We assume that these beings, having harnessed sources of energy infinitely more plentiful and efficient than our own, would also frown upon our use of such things as nuclear power, and would seek kindly to steer us away from our present destructive path, favoring instead a sort of enlightenment that arrives concomitant with the attainment of more advanced sciences. To be fair, there are also those who have warned about the dangers associated with an aggressive, colonialist civilization that might seek to conquer, enslave, or destroy mankind. Fears such as these no doubt fueled the words of physicist Stephen Hawking, who famously said in 2010 that:

We only have to look at ourselves to see how intelligent life might develop into something we wouldn't want to meet. I imagine [aliens] might exist in massive ships...having used up all the resources from their home planet. Such advanced aliens would perhaps become nomads, looking to conquer and colonize whatever planets they can reach.[1]

Hawking is to be commended for guessing about the potential threats that might accompany some non-human technological presence. Indeed, the use of systems for Messaging Extraterrestrial Intelligences (METI, or "Active SETI, " as it is sometimes also called) could present grave threats to humankind, should we inadvertently manage to signal our presence to a hostile or otherwise opportunistic alien race that might seek to exploit our resources to their advantage. However, there are other potentials worthy of consideration here, too. Far less often do we see mention of things that might exist outside the classic misperceptions and bold assumptions we've made about "alien life." Specially, what if we were to consider the presence of a robotic intelligence—not entirely unlike Saberhagen's *Berserkers*—that would be incapable of making decisions in the best interest of living organisms, based on the limitations (or advantages, depending on whose perspective we're considering) of their artificial logic?

Researchers who publicly discuss theories along these lines may remain in the minority, for now. However, there are at least a few who have taken steps to pose ideas regarding the potential interrelationship between technological Singularity, post-Singularity civilizations elsewhere in the universe, the dangers associated with SETI and METI operations, and even the risks associated with human-alien contact in general. One of these individuals, Alexei Turchin, a Russian Transhumanist and expert on global catastrophes, uses Bayesian logic to determine existential risks associated with a variety of different subjects. The term *Bayesian* refers to the English mathematician Thomas Bayes, who presented a theorem relating to probabilities associated with different sets of possible causes for an observed outcome, in which he argued that the likelihood of an outcome could be discerned based on knowledge of the causes, and the probability of each.[2] In short, this allows the user to determine the probability of an outcome, while remaining open to a variety of different potential factors that could influence it.

Interestingly, in his study of various potential global catastrophes, Turchin has also employed a Bayesian approach to a thorough assessment of the UFO enigma. This is detailed in his essay on UFOs as a global risk, which the author has made available online for download.[3] In it, Turchin discusses the concept of technological Singularity, especially in relation to potential nonhuman intelligences that may exist behind UFOs:

> [Whether] these beings may be post-singular— that is, with intelligence infinitely superior to man—remains an open question.... [I]n general, the existence of UFOs as some special [variety of]

beings should not only mean a new form of life, but also the existence of a new medium for the dissemination of information and energy.[4]

Also, with direct relevance to the idea, mentioned previously, that METI and Active SETI practices could "invite" harmful nonhuman intelligences to visit Earth, Turchin has a few more thoughts:

> We may encounter [the potential for] a SETI attack (i.e. an upload of hostile Artificial Intelligence, which uses our planet [and its resources] for future replication)...or we will attract their attention through our actions...similar to how, [using] radio METI, we could draw the attention of aliens from outer space.[5]

Finally, Turchin also addresses the potential avenues by which some highly advanced (and perhaps artificial) intelligence—in essence, a kind of *super-intelligence*—might be capable of harming humanity through its actions:

> The main feature of super-intelligence is that it is not tied to its carrier. As a result, if we are talking about the intelligence of a substance or of a computer, we immediately have in mind that this is a limited intellect...[but] intellect is a versatile weapon. If a *superhuman* intellect wants to do us harm, it will have thousands of ways to do it—from entering our computer networks, to the application of unknown physical effects.[6]

Despite the obscure nature of his research (in addition to the occasional challenge presented by our rather minimal language differentials), I found Turchin's research and various theories to be broad and insightful in their scope. Following a series of correspondences via e-mail, in October 2011 Turchin was kind enough to allow me to interview him on the subject of different risks that pertain to UFOs, as well as the kinds of advanced technology associated with their presence[7]:

Author: Given your thoughts on UFOs, what are the greatest risks you feel may be associated with their presence?

Turchin: The greatest risk is, above all, human extinction. So we should ask, first of all, whether this phenomenon could somehow lead to that. And the main risk *sources* relating to the UFO phenomenon are its unknown aspects. If we knew for certain what UFOs were, we might somehow be able predict the potential dangers associated with them. And please note that when I refer to the UFO "phenomenon," I mean that I don't know whether it constitutes alien beings, military activities, or natural phenomenon.

The risk factors are aggravated further by the fact that the phenomenon seems to have several properties that could potentially cause death and global destruction. First, there is some obvious form of intelligence that the phenomenon demonstrates, and which (may be) nonhuman in its logic. And yet, there are occasions where what we see appears to be an incomplete, or perhaps a very different intelligence that exists behind aspects of the phenomenon. Some might say it acts a little stupid, at times! Consider, for example, the Men in Black, who seem to try to mimic normal humans with their actions, but often fail. A nonhuman logic, paired with what we might call a slight "stupidity," could be a very dangerous combination. Many earthly criminals end up acting violently, simply because they don't know how to go about getting money any other way, and because they don't have compassion for other people.

The second property is the powerful source of energy employed by this phenomenon. It also has a unique ability to penetrate virtually all areas of the globe, and even some apparent ability to change or influence people's thoughts. These factors suggest an ability that UFOs may have to cause catastrophe on a global scale.

But perhaps the strongest source of risk is that, soon, humanity itself will meet thresholds that were previously unknown to us. Our technologies are growing and expanding very rapidly, and maybe as soon as within the next 20 years, this could bring us very close to discovering the true nature of the UFO phenomenon. For example, if we begin to create our own nanotechnology, we could thus increase our ability to detect alien nanotech just as well. For all we know, humanity's capabilities may eventually even exceed those of the phenomenon, and it could react to this in unpredictable ways. Obviously, no one wants to lose his or her dominance over a given situation.

Author: Do you feel UFOs are terrestrial, extra-terrestrial, interdimensional, or a variety of different things?

Turchin: I try not to "feel" anything really, and instead keep my mind open. I use a Bayesian approach, which allows for many hypotheses to exist. But my personal feeling is that UFOs are not alien spaceships with pilots inside them. Any civilization that could travel from one star system to another likely wouldn't need to send physical, flesh-and-blood "pilots."

I prefer the idea that UFOs are connected with the quantum nature of our world; they are like Schrödinger's cat, which could exist only under conditions of low concentration of the attention of its observers. This could explain why many attempts at taking UFO photos seem to fail, or end up looking like hoaxes. It could also explain how they are connected with our unconscious mind.

Author: What sorts of risks might be associated with alien nanotechnology? Could the same risks remain present if UFOs were found to be terrestrial vehicles, or even something like interdimensional phenomena?

Turchin: One risk involves another part of Transhumanist thought, which pertains to the idea of self-replicating nanorobots that could be created in Earth's near future, perhaps as soon as 2030 or 2040. These could be used in fields such as medicine, manufacturing, and even warfare. Clouds of nanobots could be used to create what we might call "clever matter," which could conceivably take any form or function. Obviously, an alien civilization would have developed nanobots long before it began to travel to different star systems. Hence, we could ask: Is it possible that we may find alien nanotechnology somewhere in the solar system, and if the answer is yes, then what will it look like, and how will it behave? Individual nanobots would be very small, and even if there were a lot of them, say, in a single room, for instance, I wouldn't be able to find them myself without using similar nanotechnology. But if they unite in the form of a "clever matter," they could take virtually any form—and here, one could ask about the seemingly ever-changing forms UFOs seem to take—maybe some are clouds of alien nanorobots?

For the time being, this is just an idea, and it can't explain all manifestations of the UFO phenomenon. Taking a different perspective now, if UFOs are some kind of secret military technology, they could be used as a means of transportation for nuclear weapons or other instruments of war; and the world seems less stable with such unpredictable and potentially dangerous technology, hence the risks this scenario might present.

Finally, if we speak about interdimensional phenomenon, we should distinguish between material "air ships" from another three-dimensional world like our own, and the potential existence of "multi-dimensional beings." In the first case, beings like us could bring such things as harmful bacteria from another world, which could eat away at our biosphere. In the second case, multi-dimensional beings could behave in relation to us like capricious gods, or like a child in a meadow that plays with ants; she may not harm them at first, but she could easily destroy their entire anthill, if any single ant were to bite her.

Author: What are your general feelings about physical anomalies and time travel?

Turchin: I think that many physical anomalies, if they do exist, have the same general qualities and physical aspects shared by UFOs.

And I don't believe in the possibility of time travel, but maybe I am just too conservative. I do encourage people to download and read my e-book, *UFOs as Global Risk*, where I give a full list of my hypotheses that could be used to explain the phenomena, as well as the risk assessment for each.

Author: In terms of being a cultural phenomenon, what role do you think UFOs play in our reality as humans?

Turchin: UFOs are a reflection of our fears. They represent a certain kind of taboo, and are often a scapegoat in the absence of real science. Unfortunately, they have also become useful as a sort of "freak test"; someone can easily be labeled a nut if he or she shows any interest in the subject. Therefore, UFOs are often used to test the edges of our rationality, or our ability to rationally and soberly look into the unknown.

Author: You've been described as a Transhumanist. Do ideas regarding technological Singularity where technology merges with humanity, the likes of which Ray Kurzweil, Vernor Vinge, and others have described, interest you, and do you feel they could be related somehow to UFOs?

Turchin: Yes, I am a Transhumanist. I think that in the near future, we will see the appearance of several super-technologies that will change the Earth as we know it today. These are nanotechnology, biotech, and, most important of all, artificial intelligence. Together, these technologies will either bring immortality to humankind, or they may just as well yield a global catastrophe; it depends entirely on how we will use these technologies.

Unfortunately, the fields of Transhumanism and UFO studies exist separately at present, but each field is capable of bringing new ideas to the other. For example, the Transhumanist Nick Bostrom created (and has mathematically proven) a theory that involves how the reality we live inside is very much like a computer simulation. And if we live in such a simulation, there could be occasional "glitches in the Matrix," as well as "Agent Smiths," or even *computer viruses*; perhaps we would perceive these as UFOs and their related phenomena. It's one of many possible hypotheses.

In early 2012, I shared a similar conversation along these lines with researcher Nigel Kerner, author of the book *Grey Aliens and the Harvesting of Souls: The Conspiracy to Genetically Tamper with Humanity*. Like Turchin, at various times I had seen that Kerner had theorized in books and articles about how certain aspects of the UFO enigma could be related to intelligence we would expect in the advent of a technological Singularity. And although my own logical pursuits regarding UFOs differ from Kerner somewhat, particularly on the grounds that he relates UFOs and alien abduction phenomenon almost entirely to the physical presence of "grey aliens," there are still many similarities between our philosophies. For instance, Kerner believes that the so-called greys are the result of beings that have essentially *manufactured* aspects of themselves; in essence, they are immortal, but rendered soulless via the tampering that led to their present state as "biomachines."[8] The similarities between this concept, paired with the near-religious undertones of "eternal life" found among some of the Singularitarians today, are worth noting, of course. Also worth noting is the fact that, whether or not all (or any) UFOs represent extraterrestrial intelligences visiting Earth, I still would surmise that such things as distance space colonization and exploration would be virtually impossible, in the absence of technological applications on par with what we already envision for a technological Singularity.

During an interview I did in early 2012 with Kerner and his colleague John Biggerstaff, PhD, a professor of cell microbiology at the University of Tennessee at Knoxville, Kerner expressed his troubled feelings on the matter of Transhumanism and Singularity. Needless to say, his views on the matter wouldn't be very encouraging to proponents of Singularity, because Kerner's general feeling is that the same processes which led to the greys as we know them are promised to humans, just as well, in the event that we give ourselves over to the sort of soul-hacking self-manipulations promised within Transhumanism.

According to Kerner[9]:

The following is from a personal interview with Nigel Kerner and John Biggerstaff, January 14, 2012. All italics are author's emphasis.

I'm sure millions will buy into the technological Transhumanism thing because so much will be promised through it. Kurzweil and his Singularity are blood-wrenchingly cold, in terms of its prospects with the human race as I see it. It's a terrifying prospect, really. The most important thing to me is that each one of us guards *preciously* all the things that make us totally natural. The moment we put into that anything where our own auspices of control over ourselves is compromised by someone else, we have a big problem. We don't become ourselves...we are *something else*. Therefore, I believe our soul, in those terms of reference, ends.

I'm not objecting to *natural* beings in the universe. Beings that come with souls, and with information systems that are natural. What I find so terrifying is the premise of beings that are *synthetic orders of created being*, that can be sent out there, and that can create mayhem, if you like, within the natural orders of existence.

Kerner went on, discussing the dangers associated with control such nonhuman intelligences might enact, and not merely as a result of the problems rooted in Transhumanism, but looking ahead to the potential for humanity's control at the hands of intelligent extraterrestrial beings as well.

Using lab rats as an analogy, Kerner noted how, up until the time they are euthanized for purposes of scientific study, these animals are generally able to lead very happy lives that are free of want or worry. Worst of all, perhaps, is the fact that they are largely unaware that they are being kept alive and healthy for mere purposes of control—and a control system that ultimately plans for their demise. "If we are lab rats," Kerner said, "then who is big enough to tell us we are?"[10]

"Also, they are hiding," Kerner noted of this potentially dangerous intelligence, "and that's the thing that tells me this is an agenda, a *hidden* agenda, that is not for our benefit."[11]

Perhaps Kerner is right; whatever the intelligence is behind UFOs, it doesn't seem too taken with the idea of coming right out and making introductions. Could it indeed be that extraterrestrial intelligences—or for that matter, any variety of conceivable nonhuman intelligence that may eventually interact with us—would literally end up posing the greatest-ever single threat to humanity, as proposed by the likes of Turchin, Kerner, and others? Despite their differing viewpoints regarding Transhumanism and Singularity, both Kerner and Turchin warned of the inherent dangers associated with our technological "coming of age," especially in the event that other more advanced intelligences are already here in our midst. Perhaps, given the scope of the present discussion, a careful examination of the dangers associated with such things as Active SETI research, as well as the potential for malevolent technological forces at work within our universe, is not just timely. If any-thing, these may also be integral to understanding our own progress as an emerging technological civilization, and one on the cusp of tremendous and radical changes we may begin to accumulate in only the next few years. And yet, when we look beyond the intellectual confines that cosmology (or even most ufology) tends to impose, we nonetheless find a very different viewpoint toward the ongoing search for nonhuman intelligence, and, not sur-prisingly, the views held by "the other camp" are far less accepting of the extraterrestrial idea on the whole.

Evolutionist Ernst Mayr detailed a number of these qualms as far back as 1979, during a conference themed around the SETI endeavors dubbed "Extraterrestrials—Where Are They?" Mayr pointed out that the extrater-restrial hypothesis essentially rested on what he called "a flawed understanding of evolution as a deterministic process."[12] In Mayr's own words, taken from the confer-ence's proceedings:

> When one looks at [proponents of the SETI proj-ect's] qualifications, one finds that they are almost exclusively astronomers, physicists and engineers. They are simply unaware of the fact that the success of the SETI project is not a mat-ter of physical laws and engineering capabilities but a matter of biologic and sociologic factors. These, quite obviously, have been entirely left out of the calculations of the possible success of the SETI project.... [Why are] biologists, who have the

greatest expertise on evolutionary probabilities, so almost unanimously skeptical of the probability of extraterrestrial intelligence? It seems to me that this is to a large extent due to the tendency of physical scientists to think deterministically, while organismic biologists know how opportunistic and unpredictable evolution is.[13]

We must, in fairness, consider whether the damning truth, in the end, could be that unsettling reality that suggests we really *are* alone, and that the idea of there being alien life elsewhere—or life similar to ourselves, at very least—is less likely than even our renowned cosmologists are willing to accept. But even if these were the circumstances, and the physical presence of other advanced civilizations were rendered logically impossible, then one resounding question would still remain: *Where does this leave us in terms of understanding the UFO problem?*

Again, we might be called to revise our notion of what "alien" really is, if not abandon most of our anticipations regarding physical alien beings altogether. Researcher Mark A. Sheridan, in his paper "SETI's Scope: How the Search for Extraterrestrial Intelligence Became Disconnected from New Ideas About Extraterrestrials," discusses how the problem could have less to do with whether or not there are aliens, favoring instead questions regarding what alternate forms a nonhuman intelligence could be expected to take: "In one of the most important, if largely overlooked, events in SETI's history, NASA formally acknowledged the nature-based critique of SETI at its 1979 Life in the Universe conference."[14] Essentially, three points were set forth during this conference with regard to alien life:

1. That humanoids were an unlikely form for any likely extraterrestrial intelligence.

2. That there is a reasonable potential for the existence of *non-humanoid* ETs.

3. That the SETI programs of the day had largely been designed only to deal with humanoid forms of intelligence like ourselves, an issue that continues to shackle our cosmological sciences to the proverbial stony cliff of bias to this day.

To address this bias, C. Owen Lovejoy, a biological anthropologist, was invited to speak about the characteristics that might distinguish humanoid and non-humanoid intelligences. Lovejoy, rather than taking the view that "intelligence" as we know it is a defining characteristic of scientific advancement, instead posited the idea that intelligence could be a form of *adaptation*, and furthermore that this "adaptation" might be labeled *cognition* in humans. "By simply distinguishing between humanoid and non-humanoid intelligence," Sheridan writes, "Lovejoy significantly broadened the official discourse about SETI in a manner that soon exposed its anthropomorphic bias."[15]

Here, it is made painfully obvious that the variety of potentials surrounding extraterrestrial life is far more complex than even most "alien theorists" today are willing to consider. Furthermore, the burden presented by a lack of proof supporting an alien presence in our midst should make this quite evident by now. But, again, what are we to make of the curious unidentified saucers, triangles, horseshoes, chevrons, and amorphous globes of energy that so many claim to have seen flying throughout our skies? Again, we are dealing with *some variety* of highly advanced technology and one that, despite the apparent and occasional "stupid" skylarking they undertake (to borrow my Russian colleague Mr. Turchin's terminology), remains capable of thwarting our best efforts at determining precisely what they are.

What we are left with are the known factors: the varieties of different UFO craft appear to represent some sort of physical, or at very least, *quasi-physical* presence. They are physical enough, at least, to be able to produce measurable amounts of electromagnetic and non-ionizing radiation, as well as highly visible, often intense sources of light. These craft also appear to be intelligently controlled. Finally, the preponderance of UFO reports that involve nuclear facilities and weapons sites seem to indicate that they are very interested in the political and military happenings within the jurisdictions of our major superpowers. They seem to actively monitor and, at times, display capabilities that allow them to overreach or even *disable* various military weapons systems.

Quite obviously, "they" are *heavily* invested in earthly happenings and perhaps have far more at stake here on this planet than most would ever guess. And this is for

one simple reason, which constitutes an entirely different set of complex circumstances and potentials that lead
toward our full understanding of the UFO presence. It is
evidenced, almost entirely, by the importance they project at the rest of the world through their mighty actions.
In short, *they act as though the very future of this planet
relied on them.*

For all we know, maybe it does.

Chapter 8

The Operators:

Memories of the Future

*If the UFO phenomenon is generated by
Earth itself, perhaps it uses the human
nervous system as a kind of operating
system. Its enduring physicality argues
that it can manipulate consciousness in
such a way that individuals can function
as unwitting projectors. If so, the study
of UFOs might eventually lead to a new
understanding of the role of awareness.
One day, through careful back-engineering
of our own minds, we might employ UFO-
like abilities through thought alone—in
which case the UFO phenomenon risks
becoming obsolete.*

—Mac Tonnies,
The Cryptoterrestrials

For the most part, the views that have been expressed with this book, *The UFO Singularity*, have largely been positive, or at least neutral in their approach to understanding what technology may be underlying the UFO phenomenon. There are a vast number of potentials that may await humanity in terms of our eventual introduction to nonhuman intelligence, and despite whether this ends up being some form of alien intelligence, or perhaps an artificial variety that we manage to create ourselves, the hopeful expectation that such changes in our eminent future will be for the better also seems to be shared by most of those in the Transhumanist realm with whom I've corresponded and interviewed. However, there do remain a number of potentials that bear the promise of a far darker outcome.

In February 2012, my weekly *Gralien Report Podcast* featured an interview with Ben Goertzel, PhD, an advisor to the Singularity Institute for Artificial Intelligence, and arguably one of the preeminent A.I. experts living today. I joked with Goertzel during our interview that, because he may be the most likely candidate for implementing artificial intelligence using computer science in the near future, he may also be one of the most dangerous men in the world. Though my commentary had obviously been tongue in cheek, Goertzel did go on to express a few concerns of his own, with his apprehensions juxtaposed alongside the overt optimism of his colleague Ray Kurzweil:

> [Kurzweil] really views the Singularity like life as it is now, but better, with no material aging, no scarcity and disease, no need to work, and a lot of amazing wish fulfillment, where humans and A.I.s work together and cyborgically fuse together, and everything's wonderful. I think that's a real possibility, and I hope it works out that way. I think there are also darker possibilities, in the sense that A.I.s could be created that see no need for human beings—and are much more powerful than human beings—with predictable consequences. But I wouldn't want to obsess on those kind of dystopian science fiction possibilities, either. The main feeling I have more strongly than Ray, it seems, is that once we hit Singularity, we just have no way to tell what's going to happen. This was Vernor Vinge's original notion of technological Singularity when he proposed it. Vinge saw it as a point after which the human mind just couldn't predict with any reliability.[1]

It is certainly interesting that, with the furtherance of human technology, we also seem to draw ever closer to the potential for extermination of our species on a large scale. During his lifetime, Carl Sagan utilized his influence in the media as a leading voice within the scientific establishment to warn about the grave potentials afforded us by the proliferation of nuclear weapons.

Goertzel, among others, similarly looks with caution at the potentials that might exist beyond that great "event horizon" that science fiction author Vernor Vinge called *technological Singularity* so many years ago. And with little doubt, Vinge himself is probably a bit tired of having to mull over the potentials for eminent disaster by now; although he acknowledged my requests for an interview on the subject, he gracefully declined discussing the topic with me, at least presently, for inclusion in this book.

But within the jurisdictions afforded us with the advent of Transhumanism, there are yet other potentials that may be of concern. Though Goertzel speculates about the dangers of A.I. that may eventually come to view humans as inferior, those same potentials might exist with regard to nonhuman intelligence from elsewhere, and regardless of whether it could be likened to what we would view as artificial. Perhaps any highly advanced alien race we may come into contact with would appear organic in nature, and yet, if the technology underlying their own existence were superior enough, it may effectively mask the fact that this apparent "race" had manufactured origins of their very own. At what point does "artificial" intelligence become indistinguishable from "natural" intelligence?

Perhaps an even more terrifying and paradigm-shifting potential would involve human origins, and the potential that life here on Earth could have resulted from some variety of cosmic seeding or tampering in ancient prehistory. For all we know, humankind and the "natural" intelligence that we seem to possess could actually be the remnant of some ancient experiment, where the intended result had been to create a new form of physical, though no less manufactured intelligence. In essence, *humans could be a form of artificial intelligence just as well*, having become divorced over the eons from the operative intelligence that created us. Our own inherent biology, and the evolutionary processes that govern what we are becoming as we grow and change as a species, may deeply color the trends that emerge within our sciences through time. For all we know, the progression of different forms of sentient consciousness throughout the cosmos may be the result of different intelligences—some of them physical, and others manifesting in far less conventional forms and states of being—as they unknowingly fulfill an innate process of self-replication, in which we go about a programmed set of tasks that will ultimately result in the next stage in cosmic evolution. Humanity may not represent the lonely island of thinkers set adrift amid the cosmos that we often perceive ourselves as being; we may instead be a mere step along the ascent toward a cosmic evolutionary lineage, in which the varieties of intelligent life that we eventually create will move forward, bearing the torch of sentient universal knowledge that was handed to them, perhaps inadvertently, by us.

Whatever the case may really be, it can hardly be argued that our innate fascination with nonhuman intelligence seems to stem from our own confusion about the mysteries of our ancient past, and what elements seemed to influence early humans the greatest in terms of our evolution. It's no surprise how often this concept of chasing human origins, or even that of A.I., and finally, extraterrestrial "controllers" working from behind the scenes, filter into our pop culture. No finer example of this exists at present, perhaps, than director Ridley Scott's film *Prometheus,* in which all these elements are fitted together intricately within a highly dystopian theme, to borrow again from Goertzel's earlier words of caution. *Prometheus* supposes that life on Earth began as a result of seeding by a race of alien beings called the "Engineers," which later prove to be a sort of menace to humankind once we eventually go looking for them. Writer Damon Lindelof, concerning the scope of the film, spoke about the way that exploration, as well as humanity's pursuit of itself and its origins, became a key theme in the writing process:

> Space exploration in the future is going to evolve into this idea that it's not just about going out there and finding planets to build colonies. It also has this inherent idea that the further we go out, the more we learn about ourselves. The characters in [Prometheus] are preoccupied by the idea: what are our origins?[2]

Greatly inspired by the work of Erich von Däniken, *Prometheus* borrows obvious influence from existent UFO and ancient astronaut literature. But despite those influences that do draw from real life, at times we must still remind ourselves that a film such as this is only fantasy, and represents merely a sci-fi space romp in which the

greatest time-tested mechanism for human destruction—
that of innate curiosity—leads to the potential extermination of our species at the hands of hostile aliens. The
reason for drawing these sorts of proverbial lines in the
sand is because, in truth, we do always manage to catch
ourselves asking how likely this scenario could really
be, or if it is even feasible at all, with the underlying
fear that in some way, shape, or form, the events portrayed in films like *Prometheus* might actually bear some
relevance to what our real future actually holds for us.
Will our own interest in the various studies of A.I., space
exploration, and alien cosmology of this sort ever really
lead us into a trap where chasing our origins could initiate
our undoing?

More likely, perhaps, is the distinct possibility that,
although nonhuman intelligence may not be intent on
destroying other forms of life such as ourselves, there
nonetheless could be some aspect of our existence—or
even several—that fall under the jurisdictions of *control*
from outside sources. I return to a single, sparing idea—
inconsequential in its delivery, but eloquent and profound
in effect—that I came across early in the research phase
for this book, where the *New York Times* had been actively
crowd-sourcing ideas about the future from its readers.
One of these ideas, which I included earlier, stood
out enigmatically amid the rest: the otherwise-fanciful
proposition that, by around the year 2100, scientists would
learn that the universe is actually a digital simulation and
that efforts were underway to contact the operators.

A wise and dear friend of mine, Dr. Maxim Kammerer of New York, once related a curious story to me. In it, he had been working in a university library, when he suddenly was taken with the notion that somewhere, amid the piles and stacks of books and classic volumes the library held, he might discover a written signature of J.R.R. Tolkien. Asking his associate nearby about this, he was advised that, although it may be a remote possibility, the likelihood of finding such a signature would be overwhelming, given the tremendous amount of material one would need to sift through. And despite this, Maxim confidently moved over toward one of the stacks of volumes nearby, and withdrew a certain book, which of course, upon opening to a random page, led to his discovery of a hand-penned signature, belonging to none other than the famous author of *The Lord of the Rings*.

I asked whether Kammerer thought this instance might have exemplified some variety of latent psychic abilities on his part. To this, he replied that, quite the contrary, when one begins to accept the pliable nature of space and time, the logic-oriented operations underlying our universe, which obviously may mirror that of computer programming and simulations, will begin to become far more apparent. Kammerer offered that, in essence, reality may have aspects that could be likened to our use of a search engine, and this sort of process might explain a wide variety of different observable phenomena.

In addition to unique and fascinating perspectives of his own, Dr. Kammerer frequently urged me to think beyond the conventional limits of the known sciences, often recommending the written works of his colleague, ufologist Jacques Vallee. In his classic book *Dimensions: A Casebook for Alien Contact,* Vallee spoke about whether there could exist what he likened to being "a spiritual control system" that might underlie much of our perception of the known universe and, of course, strange phenomena:

> I propose that there is a spiritual control system for human consciousness and that paranormal phenomena like UFOs are one of its manifestations. I cannot tell whether this control is natural and spontaneous; whether it is explainable in terms of genetics, of social psychology, or of ordinary phenomena—or if it is artificial in nature, under the power of some superhuman will. It may be entirely determined by laws that we have not yet discovered.[3]

Computational logic and computer science, I would argue, may bear a far greater similarity to any potential "artificial control system," the likes of which Vallee posits here, especially one that is seemingly "determined by laws that we have not yet discovered."[4] And yet, as intriguing as this notion that there could be, to borrow an earlier term, *operators* capable of manipulating our human perceptions of space and time through advanced simulation or other mechanisms, Vallee warns that this concept should not be misinterpreted as being an excuse for the negation of free will at the hands of, to borrow his words, some superhuman will. He goes on to say that

[w]hen I speak of a spiritual control system I do not mean that some higher supercivilization has locked us inside the constraints of a space-bound jail, closely monitored by entities we might call angels or demons. What I do mean is that mythology rules at a level of our society over which normal political and intellectual trends have no real power. At that level, time frames are long and evolution is slow.... Human life is ruled by imagination and myth; these obey strict laws and they, too, are governed by control systems, although admittedly not of the hardware type. If UFOs are acting at the mythic and spiritual level it will be almost impossible to detect it by conventional methods.[5]

Therefore, at least by Vallee's determinations expressed here, it might be the case that the influences of a sort of super-intelligence on our lives could best be evidenced through our own mythologies and cultural motifs. And thus, as Vallee correctly argues, an unconventional approach may indeed become a necessity, in terms of better understanding the source of that influence. And yet, the mystery underlying all this may not be so simple and blunt as the literal notion that our mythologies stem from physical interactions ancient humans may have had with extraterrestrial beings, as proposed in films like *Prometheus* and various literature dealing with ancient astronaut theories. Just the same, it may be that UFOs, in a general sense, are as misleading by their nature as any hazy mythology; at least when viewed in terms of trying to apply what we recognize as normal human logic toward understanding them. And even in the event that there are control systems in place, let alone aspects of the phenomenon that are geared toward some variety of *conditioning* with regard to humanity, these possibilities become very difficult to discern or decipher, though Vallee expressed thoughts in these areas just as well, in addition to ideas on how they could be applied to the future of UFO research:

> How can we verify whether such conditioning is in fact operating? We should firmly establish the primary effects. We should go on analyzing landing traces, interviewing witnesses and "abductees," feeding computers with sighting details, and scrutinizing the heavens with cameras and radio telescopes. But this activity will be completely useless if it is not related to an investigation of the secondary impact, the shift in our worldview that the phenomenon produces. A phenomenon that denies itself, that annihilates evidence of itself, cannot be mastered by engineering brute force.[6]

Although as a researcher I try to leave emotion out of the equation as much as possible, the last line that Vallee offers here strikes a particular chord: "A phenomenon that denies itself, that annihilates evidence of itself, cannot be mastered by engineering brute force."[7] In other words, it becomes painfully obvious that sometimes even the full-on, hard scientific approach to studying the UFO phenomenon is, by design, capable of nothing less than falling short when operating on its own. We can carry on collecting and analyzing data all day, every day, for another several decades, the way UFO researchers have already been doing since the end of the Second World War, but if we don't carefully take into consideration such things as the way culture, spirituality, mythology, and, of course, the limitations of human logic may influence our study of the phenomenon, we will almost inevitably remain at an intellectual stalemate with ourselves, and thus incapable of making any real progress.

Throughout the years, I have been made privy to a number of odd stories regarding such things as alien abduction, physical sightings of unusual aircraft, mystical experiences that seemed to involve contact with sapient alien intelligences, and a host of other unusual circumstances. A majority of books that deal with this subject matter, especially those having to do with how each relates to the UFO question, rely heavily on the gathering of eyewitness data, and the careful, at times even rigid categorization of elements of the encounter, based on that data. For decades now, investigative organizations and committees have compiled and painstakingly worked to preserve this information, so that a body of evidence might begin to develop, from which a new perspective might eventually emerge.

Though knowledge is certainly key to any eventual understanding one may hope to obtain from any observed phenomenon, there are times where I have felt nonetheless that the approaches to studying UFOs, in terms of investigational procedure, accepted classifications of various UFO phenomena, and other widely accepted elements of their study, have overshadowed the enigma itself. It begins to appear, at times, that many UFO researchers are so taken with the act of gathering data about sightings and compiling this information in databases that we forget to look carefully enough at the clues this data may provide. The research is thus void of any real hope of trying to reach a further understanding of its cause, because the "mission" of having categorized and ordered dates, times, places, and descriptions prior to posting them to an online database has been achieved. Sadly, the research often goes no further than this. I am reminded of the words of the careful mother who advises her daughter on the romantic advances of a potential suitor by saying: "Don't allow the letters, or the flowers, to win your heart. Give yourself to the man who loves you, and not the one who is merely in love with the thought of being in love." Perhaps there are more than a few researchers out there who are so caught up in the romantic thrill of chasing UFOs that the actual research begins to fall to the wayside.

By the same token, I could also argue in the defense of these researchers, somewhat, by admitting that an invisible target is awfully hard to shoot. UFO craft aren't best known for putting themselves out in the open for all to see, and thus, it is also understandable, to some degree, why so much emphasis is rested on the processes of data compilation. I believe that Collin Bennett may have said it best when he noted, "As any secret agent will tell us, the secret of success in this profession is not to look like James Bond, but to look like absolutely nothing at all. This is the secret of invisibility."[8] Bennett's wisdom doesn't end there, however. In fact, his musings on the current state of UFO research are perhaps some of the finest in terms of characterizing the underlying aliment, and not merely the overt symptoms:

> There is a need to construct a New Ufology which gets away from the passive listing of countless case histories from the past. Ufological studies should be integrated with the latest developments in psychology and mathematics, along with up-to-date Postmodern views on Artificial Intelligence and Image Processing.[9]

Sharing these sentiments, it was with similar reasoning in mind that I chose, with this book, to focus on the potential technological developments of the *future*, rather than to solely examine case histories and past analyses. Granted, with this book we have spent a good bit of time discussing the way expected future technologies could have already been developed elsewhere in the universe, or even here on Earth, for that matter. We've looked at how the resultant civilizations could fit into the framework surrounding the greater UFO mystery. Then again, we have also spent time looking back to mystery airships of the late 19th and early 20th centuries, as well as that most pivotal period in our history, the Second World War, during which the necessity for technological advancement may have served as the catalyst for the beginnings of a host of highly advanced, "futuristic" technologies. My reasons for doing this, however, are nonetheless geared toward understanding a few key factors that may very likely be underlying the greater UFO phenomenon. For one, looking at the potential existence of advanced aviation technology more than a century ago outlines the ways that *independent private operations* might exist behind the technology witnessed in at least some UFO reports, rather than just circumstances involving the ever-ubiquitous "they," which we assume, largely, to be government entities. (For a more thorough analysis of subversive private operations related to UFOs, and the potential for so-called "breakaway civilizations," review the written works of authors Joseph P. Farrell and Richard Dolan.) In other cases, it may simply have been that the beginnings of certain advanced scientific innovations had their genesis during a period such as World War II; if the latter were indeed the case, and what we might call "flying saucer technology" has its roots in this era—an idea that many have proposed through the years—then a strong argument for the careful suppression of this technology can also be made.

I have, on occasion, even received a few startling stories from people who have contacted me, which seemed to hint at suppression along these lines. Granted, I can hardly speak to the veracity of any such claims, knowing full well the kinds of things some people will say and do for attention (particularly in this field of research). In at least one instance, an individual who had been in contact with me about a vivid UFO encounter she and another witness had shared several years beforehand, made the claim that she had been approached by an individual in plainclothes attire, much like the various classic encounters with alleged Men in Black seen throughout UFO literature. The witness claimed that this strange man *specifically* told her "not to share any more information with Micah Hanks," with further promise that if she did, she would be visited again. Needless to say, the witness requested anonymity, and after being told this otherwise rather fanciful series of events, the individual who shared the story with me made no further attempts at contact. Admittedly, this tale bears more than just a passing resemblance to the sorts of MIB encounters related by the likes of John Keel and, more recently, researcher Nick Redfern in his book *The Real Men in Black*. I'm left to guess whether the incident really occurred or not, whether the witness was indeed "visited" again, and whether there really might be groups or individuals out there seeking to silence the claims of UFO witnesses.

Though this certainly could be a probable scenario, at least a few of the reasons a group might do this have indeed been made clear already. Returning again to the work of Nick Redfern, this time as outlined in his book *On the Trail of the Saucer Spies*, it was a concern among many intelligence officials, especially during the Cold War years, that some UFO researchers might actually be using their apparent interest in extraterrestrial phenomenon as a cover, while their real interest could be aimed at obtaining secret information about advanced air craft, which might later be passed along to enemy nations.[10] For obvious reasons, this would have been a *very* legitimate concern, especially given the pressure and paranoia that stemmed from what, at the time, were realistic threats of mutually assured destruction during that era.

And yet, although I've made it clear already that I don't attribute the entirety of my hope in unraveling the UFO mystery to extraterrestrial sources, my interest in the activities of secret aircraft is also cursory, at very best. I would not debate, of course, the tantalizing nature of any idea involving secret aircraft resembling saucers, or even the ominous, silent triangles whose shadow alone could darken entire football fields, being produced here on Earth. However, if this were the ultimate truth underlying the UFO enigma, and I were suddenly exposed to this clandestine knowledge sometime today or tomorrow, I would no doubt accept it—perhaps loudly retorting something akin to "I told you so"—and then move on.

Of far greater philosophical interest to me are the *other* potentials tucked away within the study of UFOs, which are far broader than anything as simple or obvious as the old "we built them" or "they traveled here from Zeta Reticuli" arguments. To pursue these, of course, would become a speculative endeavor, at least in part, but that hasn't seemed to thwart our progress much yet within the context of this present essay. Whether or not my reasoning will bear any fruit, perhaps time will tell— though I warn readers now that my intended meaning here, especially with regard to how *time* may be involved, could be somewhat misleading at the outset. If you will, I kindly ask that you humor me just a while longer.

On account of the observed effects of things such as time dilation, which we discussed previously, we know that the real, physical nature of time is not the observed constant that it appears to be, at least relative to human perception. In theory, aspects of what we would recognize chronologically as "the future" do already exist. So why, then, are humans incapable of perceiving such things, perhaps as literal "memories" of the future? Arguably, our limited ability to perceive certain aspects of what we refer to as "time" stem from our existence as three-dimensional, biological organisms. We are trapped within a perceptual illusion, which we recognize as being an ongoing chronological progression through the world around us that continues throughout the course of our lives. Though we seldom think about it, we are innately influenced by a variety of forces that exist in our universe, and by the manner in which those forces act on our physiology, and even our consciousness.

In his book *A Brief History of Time,* Stephen Hawking makes a few brilliant points regarding what he calls "The Arrow of Time," and how thermodynamic principles might be used to explain why human perceptions of time only tend to work with regard to our ability to perceive memories of the past. To illustrate this, he begins by explaining the known processes by which a computer stores information, and then relates this to entropy, and finally to the likely processes comprising human cognition and memory:

Before an item is recorded in a computer's memory, the memory is in a disordered state, with equal probabilities for the two possible states... after the memory interacts with the system to be remembered, it will definitely be in one state or the other, according to the state of the system.... So the memory has passed from a disordered state to an ordered one. However, in order to make sure that the memory is in the right state, it is necessary to use a certain amount of energy...this energy is dissipated as heat, and increases the amount of disorder in the universe. One can show that this increase in disorder is always greater than the increase in order of the memory itself. Thus the heat expelled by the computer's cooling fan means that when a computer records an item in memory, the total amount of disorder in the universe still goes up. The direction of time in which a computer remembers the past is the same as that in which disorder increases.

Our subjective sense of the direction of time, the psychological arrow of time, is therefore determined within our brain by the thermodynamic arrow of time. Just as a computer, we must remember things in the order in which entropy increases.[11]

Hawking goes on to argue, based on the weak anthropic principle, that the very existence of intelligent life like ourselves must rely on the universe being in a state of expansion through time. In this state, the universe grows outward, trending ever more toward a state of disorder as time progresses. "Thus," Hawking says:

...intelligent life could not exist in the contracting phase of the universe. This is the explanation of why we observe that the thermodynamic and cosmological arrows of time point in the same direction. It is not that the expansion of the universe causes disorder to increase. Rather, it is that the no boundary condition causes disorder to increase and the conditions to be suitable for intelligent life only in the expanding phase."[12]

This brings to mind a very interesting question. In the event that certain aspects of entropy could be reversed or nullified, and more specifically, through technology that changed these sorts of things relative to an individual, how would such a being be capable of perceiving time? If a physical being could harness the literal ability to prevent the entropic processes that govern their perception of time and overall longevity—in other words, if they could achieve immortality—then how might their perception of time change, or would it?

In truth, immortality alone may not be enough to do the trick. The physical processes underlying cognitive activities expend far more energy, and thus *increase* universal disorder, than the order that is achieved by functions of the mind such as creating a memory. What we would need, in addition to technology that would aid the reversal of entropy's influence on the physical body, would be more efficient processes that could similarly influence entropic influence on human cognition.

The concept of reversing entropy has been a point of argument since long before now; physicist Erwin Schrödinger discussed this as far back as 1943, in his book *What Is Life?*, inspiring the later use of a term Léon Brillouin created for this, which he called *negentropy*.[13] The idea of negentropy has at times also been closely linked to discussions involving free energy—which, as a brief aside, is interesting to note here if we consider the expected use of vast and limitless power sources many have proposed for the function behind various UFO craft. The connections here might strongly suggest that harnessing an ability to reverse or manipulate the effects of entropy would almost be requisite for the kinds of technologies UFOs seem to utilize. Of course, the same could be said of any other intelligent race that seeks to expand their universal horizons in such a way, and hence, humans can't be left out of the running here, either. And though we're still a good way from achieving methods of reversing entropy in order to change human physiology—or perhaps even human perception of time—when we consider many of the expected advents of Transhumanism, there may indeed be factors present that could allow us to rethink the apparent limitations entropy imposes on beings like ourselves.

Kurzweil and others within Transhumanist circles have spoken extensively of things like nanotechnology (which my colleague Alexei Turchin also mentioned briefly, in the last chapter) for use in miniaturizing computer systems and furthering human technology on the near-atomic scale. Eventually, this kind of technology will also present us with new ways we can improve ourselves as individuals, but of equal relevance to the discussion of nanotech for use in computing processes and the reversal of entropy is the concept of *reverse computation*. This could be defined as computation that manages to conserve energy by maintaining and performing operations that *preserve* a system, rather than creating entropy (released as heat) through more destructive operations, the likes of which are still in use with present-day computers. Successful demonstrations have already shown that reverse computation can be achieved, though the technology is obviously still in its infancy.[14] However, we already know from the few existing studies that the process does result in both a reduction in energy input, as well as the expected resulting decrease in heat dissipation, both of which *greatly* increase the overall efficiency of any system that may utilize such processes.

Bringing this back to the concept of nanotechnology, in his paper "A Physicist's Model of Computation," Edward Fredkin addresses why the use of microscopic components would allow a computer to operate at its absolute maximum levels of efficiency:

> If [a] computer is built out of microscopically reversible components then it can be perfectly efficient. How much energy does a perfectly efficient computer have to dissipate in order to compute something? The answer is that *the computer does not need to dissipate any energy.* [author's emphasis][15]

If a computer could, in theory, function in the complete absence of energy dissipation, we not only see broad implications in terms of so-called "free energy." We also see that future technologies may be capable of attaining processes that nearly, or even *completely* reverse natural entropy, thus increasing their efficiency. But perhaps the most fascinating potential here, of course, would involve the combination of advanced nanotechnology and reverse computation with human biology in innovative ways, thus lessening certain restrictions that may presently influence our thoughts, and even human perception, due to the laws of thermodynamics.

Although these radical promises for tomorrow's civilization are indeed fascinating, by now you still might be asking what all this could possibly have to do with bettering our understanding of UFOs. In summary, based on what we know about the function of the human mind, as well as that of computer systems and the obvious restrictions placed on each of these courtesy of the second law of thermodynamics, the reasons underlying our limited perception of time are thus revealed. As Hawking argued, the general trend toward states of disorder that prevails in our universe somewhat governs our ability to perceive time, which is thus limited to observation of the present, as well as computational data or memories of what we perceive as being "the past." The future, though no doubt existent, has not occurred yet within the limited jurisdictions of human perception. In theory, however, it might not always remain the case that humans would be bound by such physical limitations, if certain entropic forces were managed correctly. We also see that the efficiency of computers can be greatly increased—perhaps to a point of perfect efficiency where no energy is dissipated at all—on a microscopic level. This calls into question the use of future nanotechnology to improve the way that computers, and eventually the human mind, will be able to function. Ray Kurzweil has argued that a hyper-efficient supercomputer of the future (the "ultimate laptop,"[16] to borrow MIT professor Seth Lloyd's name for it) would have the capacity "to simulate one hundred thousand human brains in a cubic centimeter."[17] By the year 2030 alone, if Kurzweil is right, such computing will be "roughly equal to our estimate for the capacity of all living biological human intelligence."[18] And arguably, as the efficiency of such technology brings us closer to achieving *negentropic* computation within computers, the human mind, and even varieties of artificial intelligence, the universal influences that dictate our perception of things such as "time" may begin to change quite drastically as well.

Let us now imagine an intelligent future civilization, perhaps several centuries further along than our own. Consider the vast technological potentials they will inevitably manage to harness, the very beginnings of which we've only begun to touch on within the scope of our present discussion. To wit, I would find it highly unlikely that such a future civilization, having augmented its biology and cognitive processes, or perhaps supplanted them altogether with advanced cybernetics, would be capable of anything less than perception of levels of reality far beyond our present human abilities. By the same token, with regard to this civilization's expected ability to transcend the perceptual boundaries of time, there would probably be little necessity for the literal creation of clunky devices and machinery we would call "time machines." I would argue instead that, rather than building devices literally capable of traveling through physical time, this eventual human ability to evade temporality would be rooted largely in the *perception* of time itself, and that those in future generations might utilize such facilities to interact with other non-temporal states—states the likes of which you or I might call our present day. Also, it could be argued that at least certain aspects of this future intelligence, with capabilities allowing them to observe, or even *manipulate* time in radical ways, would occasionally manifest as phenomena perceptible to us.

Bearing this in mind, consider now the almost *ghostly* nature of many UFO reports, in which these craft move at tremendous speeds, vanish into thin air, cause strange distortions in the passage of time relative to those nearby (in other words, the phenomenon known as "missing time," as reported by many abductees), and a host of other strange phenomenon and odd occurrences. Rather than having anything to do with the strange and overt use of "magic" wielded by an apparent intelligence in our midst, perhaps these odd occurrences are merely clues—broken fragments of a larger puzzle extending toward us from beyond our own perceptual limits of space and time. We might liken each manifestation of certain UFO phenomenon to pinholes of light escaping through cracks in the cosmic barrier; they reveal brilliant streams of illumination on an occasional basis, but never enough to allow full visibility of their source.

And yet, what if we were to one day find that the source of this illumination had been human in nature all along—or at very least, that it had been rooted in some aspect *of what humans are eventually destined to become?*

Artwork by Caleb Hanks.

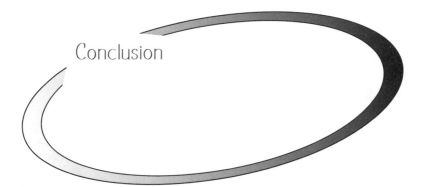

Conclusion

I am an outsider; a stranger in this century and among those who are still men. This I have known ever since I stretched out my fingers to the abomination within the great gilded frame; stretched out my fingers and touched a cold and unyielding surface of polished glass.

—Howard Phillips Lovecraft,
The Outsider, 1921

By the time we finally reach a point where our accessible technology can be utilized in determining, to some degree of conclusiveness, what varieties of phenomenon are underlying the UFO mystery, the question of their existence—which burns so strongly in our minds and culture today—may no longer bear quite the same significance that it holds for us now. Indeed, this statement may sound a bit strange, but if, in the event that some UFO craft were found to be originating from our future, or from secret technology already in our midst, or from outer space—or from *anyplace else,* for that matter—by the time we have technologies that would allow us to recognize or study these, our own technological capabilities will likely be nearing or intersecting with "theirs"—whomever it is that "they" may turn out to be. We will have reached a singular point in our own existence, where our technology reaches upward like the curious hand of Adam toward that of his Creator, ready to grasp a new kind of knowledge, power, and insight, and merge together with it as *one,* rather than merely staring at it in awe from a safe distance.

In essence, the intellectual and technological "union" we hope would result, given the best-case scenario, with a new kind of knowledge, as well as an entirely new perspective of our universe, may greatly overshadow the discovery of another intelligence in our midst. A better way of putting it might be to liken the fate of such "alien" technology to being rendered effectively *obsolete*, to borrow again from the terminology employed by the late Mac Tonnies, which I included at the beginning of Chapter 8.

This, of course, represents a concept that I have begun to refer to as *the UFO Singularity*, a point where our own technological capabilities will become so advanced that they begin to mirror that of other intelligences in our universe, some of which may already be in our midst, though partially obscured by the limitations of human perception. Eventually, it could be argued that these two separate technologies may begin to share their discoveries with one another, and perhaps even merge together as one unified intelligence at some point. Or, in the event that hostilities may arise between them instead, perhaps they will just as simply negate each other. The likelihood of any such scenario that might arise, let alone the vast implications they might entail, presents us with considerations that extend well beyond the scope of the present discussion; they are, however, no less pivotal to our very existence, whether they are discussed here, or at a later time.

Having been rendered essentially indistinguishable from one another, we can hope that perhaps the eventual merging of two advanced intelligences, rather than manifesting as some cosmic collision between distant alien cultures, would in a way resemble the simple, yet sublime discoveries of our earliest primitive ancestor. I can imagine this curious young creature as he crept along the water's edge, searching only for those things known to him in his sheltered, but demanding little world. Perhaps he hoped to catch a fish, or to find an unattended nest full of eggs he could steal, though maybe some bright stone, which had captured the sun's brilliance from beneath the running brook, would steal his attention away occasionally.

It was here, as he hunted along the familiar banks of this shallow stream, that chasing an unexplained illumination from beneath the water's surface—one not unlike the strange lights that haunt our skies today—led him to discover a still pool, and he peered into it for the first time. There, it was nothing alien or monstrous that he found; it was merely his own likeness, captured in the water's reflection. And yet, in a sense, he had discovered something far more complex and terrifying than any water nymph, monster, or intelligent alien being lurking beneath the ripples that scattered gently across its surface.

He had discovered, for the very first time, *himself.*

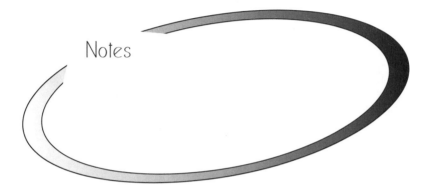

Notes

Introduction
1. Vallee, "Unidentified."

Chapter 1
1. "Things."
2. Ibid.
3. "Twenty."
4. "Predicting."
5. "15 Big."
6. "Google Effects."
7. "Google Has Made."
8. Coffman and Odlyzko, "The Size."
9. Jung, *The Archetypes.*
10. Goertzel, "When."
11. Ibid.
12. Pelletier, "Global."
13. Heinlein, *The Moon.*
14. Ibid.
15. Vinge, "First."
16. Vinge, *Threats,* p. 72.
17. Vallee and Meyer, "Dynamics."
18. "What Is?"
19. Ibid.
20. Kurzweil, *The Singularity.*

21. Fowler, *The Andreasson.*

22. Vallee, *Dimensions.*

23. Ibid.

Chapter 2

1. Strieber, *Communion.*

2. Ibid.

3. Deutsch, "Quantum."

4. Hafele and Keating, "Around-the-World."

5. Calder, *Magic*, p. 378.

Chapter 3

1. Verne, *Robur.*

2. Ibid.

3. Ibid.

4. Schnabel, *Dark.*

5. Ibid.

6. Danelek, *The Great.*

7. Nicholson, "Those?"

8. Ibid.

9. Ibid.

10. Danelek, *The Great.*

11. Dooley, "The Development."

12. Danelek and Davis, *Phantoms.*

13. Kurzweil, *The Singularity.*

14. Danelek, *The Great.*

15. Scully, *Behind.*

16. Ibid.

17. Farrell, Lecture.

18. Moiseenko, "UFO."

19. *Coast to Coast AM.*

20. All quotations in the following paragraphs recounting Stewart's story are from the *Coast to Coast AM* show.

21. Liebson, "The Discharge."

22. Watson, *Radar.*

23. All Maloney quotations from an interview with Mack Maloney, February 15, 2012.

24. Fuller, *Proceedings.*

25.

Chapter 4

1. Personal correspondence via e-mail from Dallas Michael (Mike) Reese, June 9, 2011.

2. Ibid.

3. Ibid.

4. Ibid.

5. Clark, *The UFO.*

6. Personal correspondence via e-mail from Dallas Michael (Mike) Reese, June 9, 2011.

7. Schnabel, *Dark.*

8. Personal correspondence via e-mail from Dallas Michael (Mike) Reese, June 9, 2011.

9. Ibid.

10. Personal conversation with Dallas Michael (Mike) Reese, September 24, 2011.

11. Ibid.

12. Ibid.

13. Ibid.

14. Ibid.

15. Ibid.

16. Dektar, "Additive."

17. Center, "James."

18. Maxwell, *A Treatise.*

19. Tombe, "The Unification."

20. Personal correspondence via e-mail from Dallas Michael (Mike) Reese, June 9, 2011.

21. Ibid.

22. MUFON.

23. Personal correspondence via e-mail from Dallas Michael (Mike) Reese, June 9, 2011.

24. Personal conversation with Dallas Michael (Mike) Reese, September 24, 2011.

25. Ibid.

26. Ibid.

Chapter 5

1. Gallawa, "The History."

2. This conversation with Amy from December 2011 are paraphrased from recollection of the conversation.

3. Personal correspondence with Jeff Rose, January 21, 2012.

4. Ibid.

5. Vallee, *Dimensions.*

6. Ibid.

7. Walton, *Fire.*

8. Friedman and Marden, *Captured!*

9. Tumminia, *Alien.*

10. Hanks, "Taken."

11. Steinberg, The Paracast, February 12, 2012.

12. Ibid.

13. Cannon, "The Controllers."

14. Ibid.

15. Ibid.

16. Ibid.

17. Ibid.

18. Ibid.

19. Ibid.

20. Ibid.

21. Ibid.

Chapter 6

1. Fuller, "Flying."

2. McDonald, "Science."

3. Lowe, "Some."

4. Ibid.

5. Koestler, *Janus.*

6. Sagan, speech.

7. Sagan, "Cosmos."

8. Alfred, "Plasma."

9. Ruppelt, *The Report.*

10. De Sprague, *Lovecraft.*

Chapter 7

1. "Into the Universe."

2. Jaynes, "Bayesian."

3. Turchin, "UFO."

4. Ibid.

5. Ibid.

6. Ibid.

7. Personal interview with Alexei Turchin, October 7, 2011.

8. Kerner, *Grey*.

9. Personal interview with Nigel Kerner and John Biggerstaff, January 14, 2012.

10. Ibid.

11. Ibid.

12. Zuckerman and Hart, *Extraterrestrials*.

13. Ibid.

14. Sheridan, "SETI's."

15. Ibid.

Chapter 8

1. *Gralien*, Interview.

2. Child, "Ridley."

3. Vallee, *Dimensions*.

4. Ibid.

5. Ibid.

6. Ibid.

7. Ibid.

8. Bennett, *Flying*.

9. Ibid.

10. Redfern, *On the Trail*.

11. Hawking, *A Brief*.

12. Ibid.

13. Brillouin, "Negentropy."

14. Merkle, "Reversible."

15. Fredkin, "A Physicist's."

16. Kurzweil, *The Singularity.*

17. Ibid.

18. Ibid.

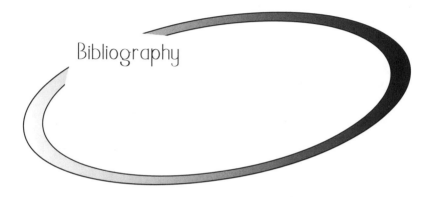

Bibliography

Alfred, Jay. "Plasma Life Forms: Dark Panspermia." Unexplained Mysteries Website. *www.unexplained-mysteries.com/column.php?id=115488.*

Bennett, Colin. *Flying Saucers Over the White House.* Cosimo Books, 2011.

Brillouin, Leon. "Negentropy Principle of Information." *Journal of Applied Physics, volume 24,* 1953: 1152–1163.

Calder, Nigel. *Magic Universe: A Grand Tour of Modern Science.* Oxford University Press, 2006.

Cannon, Martin. "The Controllers: A New Hypothesis of Alien Abduction." Monograph: 1989. *www.constitution.org/abus/controll.htm.*

Child, Ben. "Ridley Scott Beams Into Comic-Con to Unveil Prometheus." *The Guardian,* July 22, 2011.

Clark, Jerome. *The UFO Book: Encyclopedia of the Extraterrestrial.* Visible Ink Press, 1998.

Coast to Coast AM,, August 3, 2011. "UFOs on the Record" with guest Leslie Kean. *www.coasttocoastam.com/show/2011/08/03.*

Coffman, K.G., and A.M. Odlyzko. "The Size and Growth Rate of the Internet." AT&T Labs Research. Revised version, October 2, 1998.

Danelek, J. Allan. *The Great Airship of 1897*. Adventures Unlimited Press, 2009.

Danelek, J. Allan, and Chuck Davis. *Phantoms of the Skies: The Lost History of Aviation from Antiquity to the Wright Brothers*. Adventures Unlimited Press, 2011.

De Camp, L. Sprague. *Lovecraft: A Biography*. Ballantine Books, 1976.

Dektar, Katie. "Additive Versus Subtractive Color Mixing." Stanford University Online, Graphics Division. *graphics.stanford.edu/courses/cs178/applets/colormixing.html*.

Deutsch, David. "Quantum Mechanics Near Closed Timelike Curves." *Physical Review, volume 44, issue 10*, 1991: 3197–3217.

Dooley, Sean C. "The Development of Material-Adapted Structural Form." *biblion.epfl.ch/EPFL/theses/2004/2986/EPFL_TH2986_screen.pdf*.

Duff, Michael J. "The Theory Formerly Known as Strings." *Scientific American*, February 1998: 64–69.

Farrell, Joseph P. *Saucers, Swastikas and Psyops*. Adventures Unlimited Press, 2012.

Farrell, Joseph. Lecture before the International UFO Congress. Laughlin, Nevada, 2009.

"15 Big Ways the Internet Is Changing Our Brain." OnlineCollege.org Website. *www.onlinecollege.org/15-big-ways-the-internet-is-changing-our-brain*.

Fowler, Ray. *The Andreasson Affair*. Wild Flower Press, 1994.

Fredkin, Edward. "A Physicist's Model of Computation." Proceedings of the Twenty-sixth Recontre de Moriond, Texts of Fundamental Symmetries. 1991.

Friedman, Stanton, and Katleen Marden. *Captured! The Betty and Barney Hill UFO Experience*. New Page Books, 2007.

Fuller, Curtis. *Proceedings of the First International UFO Congress*. Warner Books, 1980.

Fuller, John G. "Flying Saucer Fiasco." *Look Magazine*, May 14, 1968.

Gallawa, John Carlton. "The History of the Microwave Oven." Gallawa.com Website, 1998. *www.gallawa.com/microtech/history.html*.

Goertzel, Ben. "When the Net Becomes Conscious." The Multiverse According to Ben weblog, March 10, 2009. *multiverseaccordingtoben.blogspot.com/2009/03/when-net-becomes-consciousness.html*.

"Google Effects on Memory: Cognitive Consequences of Having Information at Our Fingertips." *Science* Website, July 14, 2011. *www.sciencemag.org/content/early/2011/07/13/science.1207745*.

"Google Has Made Our Memories Lazy, Say Scientists." Daily Mail Website. *www.dailymail.co.uk/sciencetech/article-2015117/Google-stupid-How-search-engine-rewired-memory-leave-forgetful.html*.

Gralien Report Podcast. Interview with Ben Goertzel, PhD, February 2012.

Hafele, J.C., and R.E. Keating. "Around-the-World Atomic Clocks: Predicted Relativistic Time Gains." *Science, vol. 177, no. 4044,* 1972: 166–168.

Hanks, Micah. "Taken With the Night: UFO Abductions and the Human Factor." Mysterious Universe Website. *mysteriousuniverse.org/2012/01/taken-with-the-night-ufo-abductions-and-the-human-factor/.*

Hawking, Stephen. *A Brief History of Time.* Bantam, 1988.

Heinlein, Robert. *The Moon Is a Harsh Mistress.* Orb Books, 1997.

"Into the Universe With Stephen Hawking." Discovery Channel. Originally aired April 25, 2010.

"James Clerk Maxwell biography." Center for Imagine Science Website. *www.cis.rit.edu/node/280.*

Jaynes, E.T. "Bayesian Methods: General Background." Appeared in *Maximum-Entropy and Bayesian Methods in Applied Statistics,* by J.H. Justice (editor). Cambridge University Press, 1986.

Jung, Carl G. *The Archetypes and the Collective Unconscious.* Princeton, N.J.: Princeton University Press, 1981.

Kerner, Nigel. *Grey Aliens and the Harvesting of Souls: The Conspiracy to Genetically Tamper with Humanity.* Rochester, Vt.: Bear & Company, Rochester, 2010.

Koestler, Arthur. *Janus: A Summing Up.* Random House, 1978.

Kurzweil, Ray. *The Singularity Is Near.* Penguin (Non-Classics), 2006.

Liebson, S.H. "The Discharge Mechanism of Self-Quenching Geiger-Mueller Counters." *Physical Review, vol. 72, no. 7,* 1947: 602–608.

Lowe, Robert. "Some Thoughts on the UFO Project." National Investigations Committee on Aerial Phenomena Website, August 9, 1966. *www.nicap. org/docs/660809lowmemo.htm.*

Maxwell, James Clerk. *A Treatise on Electricity and Magnetism.* Nabu Press, 2010.

McClure, Kevin. "The Nazi UFO Mythos: An Investigation." *magonia. haaan.com/2009/nazi-ufo-00-intro/.*

McDonald, James E. "Science in Default: Twenty-Two Years of Inadequate UFO Investigations." American Association for the Advancement of Science, 134th Meeting. General Symposium, "Unidentified Flying Objects." December 27, 1969.

Merkle, Ralph C. "Reversible Electronic Logic Using Switches." *Nanotechnology 4,* 1993.

Moiseenko, Andrew. "UFO Croaking in the Ocean." *Pravda,* Russian Online Edition, June 20, 2006. *www.kp.ru/daily/23726/54249/.*

MUFON Georgia Witness Reports Database. *www. mufonga.org/mufongasighting.html.*

Nicholson, Andrew. "Those Mysterious Lights: Australia's First UFO Flap in 1909?" WeirdAustralia. com Website. *weirdaustralia.com/2012/03/16/those-mysterious-lights-australias-first-ufo-flap-in-1909/.*

Pelletier, Dick. "Global Brain: The Internet Could Become Conscious by Mid-2030s." Future Blogger Website, March 15, 2008. *memebox.com/futureblogger/show/158.*

"Predicting the Future of Computing." *New York Times* online, December 5, 2011. *www.nytimes. com/interactive/2011/12/06/science/20111206-technology-timeline.html?ref=science.*

Redfern, Nick. *On the Trail of the Saucer Spies.* Anomalist Books, 2006.

Ruppelt, Edward J. *The Report on Unidentified Flying Objects.* Cosimo Classics, 2011.

Sagan, Carl. "Cosmos." *Encyclopedia Galactica,* Episode 12. Original air date December 14, 1980.

Schnabel, Jim. *Dark White: Aliens, Abductions, and the UFO Obsession.* Hamish Hamilton, 1994.

Scully, Frank. *Behind the Flying Saucers.* Henry Holt & Co., 1950.

Sheridan, Mark A. "SETI's Scope: How the Search for Extraterrestrial Intelligence Became Disconnected from New Ideas About Extraterrestrials." Ph.D. thesis, Drew University. May 2009. Available online at *www.daviddarling.info/encyclopedia/S/SETI_critical_history_inflection.html.*

Steinberg, Gene. *The Paracast* (audio podcast), featuring guests Kevin D. Randle and Jim Moseley. February 12, 2012.

Strieber, Whitley. *Communion.* Beech Tree Books, 1987.

"Things Will Come to Pass of Which Man Little Dreams." *Miami Metropolis,* June 23, 1911.

Tombe, Frederick David. "The Unification of Gravity and Magnetism." *The General Science Journal,* April 22, 2007.

Tumminia, Diana G. *Alien Worlds: Social and Religious Dimensions of Extraterrestrial Contact.* Syracuse University Press, 2007.

Turchin, Alexei. "UFO as Global Risk." Version 0.910, March 30, 2010. Scribd Website.. *www.scribd. com/doc/18221425/UFO-as-Global-Risk.*

"Twenty Top Predictions for Life 100 Years From Now." BBC Website, January 16, 2010. *www.bbc.co.uk/ news/magazine-16536598.*

Vallee, Jacques. *Dimensions: A Casebook of Alien Contact.* Contemporary Books, 1988.

___. "Unidentified Aerial Phenomena: An Opportunity for Innovation." Presented before the Global Competitiveness Forum, January 31, 2011.

Vallee, Jacques, and Francois Meyer. "Dynamics of Long Term Growth." *Technological Forecasting and Social Change,* 1975.

Verne, Jules. *Robur the Conqueror.* 1886.

Vinge, Vernor. "First Word." *Omni,* January 1983: 10.

_____. *Threats and Other Promises.* Baen Books, 1988.

Walton, Travis. *Fire in the Sky: The Walton Experience. Third Edition.* Marlowe & Company, 1997.

Watson, Jr., Raymond C. *Radar Origins Worldwide: History of its Evolution in 13 Nations Through World War II.* Trafford Publishing, 2009.

"What Is the Singularity?" Singularity Institute Website. *singinst.org/overview/whatisthesingularity/.*

Zuckerman, Ben, and Michael H. Hart (editors). *Extraterrestrials – Where Are They? Second Edition.* Cambridge University Press, 1995.

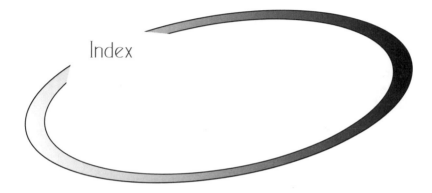

Index

About the Author

ICAH HANKS works full-time as an author, musician, journalist, and radio personality. He has contributed articles and stories regarding strange phenomenon, scientific discoveries, and political topics to publications such as *Fate, Intrepid Magazine, New Dawn, UFO Magazine,* and several other publications. In 2010, his research regarding altered states of consciousness, psychedelic drugs, and the prevalence of similarities between archetypal folklore from around the world culminated in his book *Magic, Mysticism and the Molecule: The Search for Sentient Intelligence from Other Worlds.* He has also been a contributor to several anthologies in the *Exposed, Uncovered, and Declassified* series, released by New Page Books in 2011. Hanks has appeared on numerous television and radio programs, including National Geographic's *Paranatural,* the History Channel's *Guts and Bolts,* CNN Radio, *The Jeff Rense Program,* and a variety of other shows and podcasts. He can be reached through his Website, The Gralien Report, at *www.gralien-report.com.*